DREAM
YOUR
WAY TO
SUCCESS

DREAM YOUR WAY TO SUCCESS

The story of
*Dr. Yonggi Cho
and Korea*
by

Nell L. Kennedy

Logos International
Plainfield, New Jersey

134349

All Scripture references are taken from
the King James Version unless otherwise
noted as NAS (New American Standard).

Dedicated to
Hananim
and His family
wherever they are.

Contents

Foreword

This book is the story of one man, but it is also the story of the people throughout his nation who have served as models to show me the Korea that nurtured him.

We can learn much from the Korean experiences, and one of my aims in the book is that the lifeblood of Korea would flow through the writing. It is my prayer that in these pages, the reader will also touch Jesus Christ, my Friend and my Source.

To that end, I express thanks to God through His Son, Jesus, for ordaining all of this.

In these opening pages I wish to acknowledge the help of many people.

To my friends Cho Yonggi and his beautifully sensitive wife, who have given me this opportunity of entering their lives in order to write this book.

To Jashil Choi and to her brother, Elder Choi.

To the parents of Cho Yonggi, the Elder Cho delighting my ears with tales from his memory; and to all the family members for their patience with this foreigner who pried into their lives.

To Elder Lee and the office workers at World Mission Center. The dormitory personnel and deaconesses, the drivers, and the photographer, Mr. Hong.

Deep gratitude to Dr. John Hurston, his wife, Maxine; and to Karen Hurston, their daughter, for their encouragement, advice and help; and to the staff at Church Growth International.

To Cha Il Suk and Miss Duk Hee Cha, devotedly serving, always serving; to Mr. Kim and Mr. Choi and all the *Shinange* magazine staff for helping me belong to them.

To Jack and Kathy Holm. To David and Ellen Ross, Debbie, David and Becky, who ministered to me and helped at a critical time for the book.

I am indebted to the office of the honorable Mayor of Seoul and for Deputy Mayor Kim's gracious hospitality and explanations regarding Yoido and city planning.

To Dr. George Paik and the many other knowledgeable scholars and historians who took time from their busy schedules to share valuable insights and information.

And especially in Japan, where I live, my debt of appreciation is beyond expression. I am thankful to my friends Michiko Teramoto and Hisako Mitsui, whose help, encouragement and understanding have been as a refreshing drink in a sandy desert; and to my pastor and family, the Rev. Tsugumichi Ohkawa, as well as missionary Marvin Fast and countless others. The prayers of Berni Marsh and Teruko Kawashima have been as a steadfast anchor, their unqualified love sustaining me. Naoe Toshimi helped in more ways than she will ever know.

And then, my mother, sacrificing and brave, while this daughter lives in another world an ocean away—special appreciation to her and all my family, my mother, my brother and sister, for keeping one another.

Writing is necessarily a personal involvement, and writing this book has taken a heavy toll on certain relationships. To friends who must have thought I had given them up, thanks for your patience and endurance and for your willingness to move onward.

The pages of this book cannot really end the story, for it is a how-to book on a continual learning process. It is the story of a man learning about his Father, and of a people learning about our God. And that story goes on, and on.

Nell Kennedy

Introduction

Our beloved sister, Miss Nell Kennedy, is a very devoted Christian writer who is loved dearly by many in Japan and Korea.

For a long time many people encouraged me to write my life story, but I could not develop the courage to do so, for in the Orient, it is presumptuous for a young man to write his own biography. (I was forty-two years old at that time.)

But because of the requests and encouragements of many friends overseas, I have summoned up enough courage to ask Miss Kennedy to write my story.

I do appreciate her hard work and successful writing. I have only one hope in sharing my story—that is to give all the glory to God and to encourage fellow-Christian workers through my church and ministry.

Yonggi Cho, D.D., D.Litt.
조용기 Pastor, Full Gospel Central Church
President, World Mission Association

1

Don't Spit Against the Wind

(1942-1945)

"Miss Arai, I want to marry you."

"But, Yonggi, I'm only your teacher." She smiled as her petite frame bent forward, her gentle black eyes looking into those of the six-year-old boy who stood at his teacher's side. "And anyway, I am Japanese. Let's wait until you are in the second grade next year and then see how you feel about it. Okay?"

There it was again, he thought—that Japanese air of superiority. But surely Miss Arai was different. She did not flaunt her Japanese background the way the other teachers did, constantly saying, "We Japanese!" It was the teacher Kai Sensei that everybody hated, coming every afternoon to walk away with the youthful Miss Arai; sometimes he made her cry and her nose turned red. What right did he have? She was *their* teacher. She often put her arms around the first graders, something Yonggi never remembered seeing another Japanese do. For her they would do anything.

They memorized the Japanese writing system, hundreds of characters, in one year. They studied Japanese history instead of Korean, and read Japanese folk tales and emulated old samurai heroes. Miss Arai made reasons for them to learn and originated games in which they could jump or run for arithmetic so as to keep warm in the unheated schoolhouse for Koreans. Some got their feet wet coming through the rain and occasional snow. Only the children of wealthy landowners were permitted to wear the *gomushin,* traditional white rubber shoes of Korea, as rubber was scarce. Others made do with the Japanese wooden clogs known as *geta,* while the poorest made shoes of rice straw.

It was wartime in the Pacific. It was always wartime in Korea. But no problem is so difficult as to thwart a schoolboy's hope of marrying his favorite teacher. He guessed Miss Arai to be as old as eighteen or nineteen. She lived in Mr. Murata's house on the Japanese side of the village. More than that, he knew nothing about her but that she smiled and was kind to her pupils.

There was only one other girl he loved as much, and that was Older Sister, Hae Sook. Three years ahead of him in school, she walked beside him every morning and evening, along the eerie mountain path he dreaded to climb alone.

This afternoon he would try to be brave and cross the creek without Sister's hand. More times than he could count, a wolf was lapping up a drink on the other side. Fear gripped hold of Yonggi and he grabbed Sister's hand. There it was—the bristling gray beast, his steely eyes glaring steadfastly and not moving a muscle! Yonggi in a flash squatted to pray while Sister chased the animal with a stick. "O god of water," he screamed, "please don't let the wild animals eat us up. O god of trees, keep the foxes away till we get home to Mama." Rubbing his hands together to make petition, he cried out to one more: "O god of sky, please, please don't let that hoot owl screech at us. Protect us, all the gods, please, please!"

There were so many gods in Korea, one dared not to leave any out.

A wild eagle squawked overhead as if to say, "You forgot about me, hee-hee-hee." Yonggi crouched again with hands over his head, his legs trembling as he imagined a dead man lurching in the shadows of the graveyard they had to pass. A witch would no doubt be sitting at a tomb beating her drum, having been hired by some bereaved family to appease the restless spirit of someone who had died. If a family was undergoing needless sickness or accidents, quarrels or financial worries, or if an older child wandered aimlessly into trouble or otherwise proved a disappointment to the family's expectations, the cause of such serious trouble might be connected with the deceased relative. A spirit often came back to haunt the family who did not remember the dead properly. So a family would pay a witch woman, the *mudang* of the Shamanism religion, and go with her to the cemetery to chant and pamper the ancestor spirits with sacrifice offerings of food. At a distance she was a curiosity with her loud drum and shrill flute, but it was frightening to have to walk through the cemetery while she was there. It was said that she drank a concoction of blood and insects; Yonggi doubted whether anyone got close enough to tell. But he had seen her burning incense and wailing for over an hour at one grave. The better the offerings, the better the wailing, as the sorceress took the offerings later as her fee. To Yonggi, her wailing sounded exactly like the eagle's and he wondered whether she turned into some kind of beast when she was not busy with her trade. Just to be safe, he stopped and bowed, clasped his hands together and in rapid mumbles got a prayer off to the tombs, then made a blind dash for the other side of the graveyard before stopping to catch his breath.

Every day they spent three hours on the winding, willowy trail, there being no shorter way to and from school. Sometimes Sister ran far enough ahead to coax him on; other times she gave him her hand to pull him up the steep places. Sister had made a path as a result of three years of going to school by herself. It was fun now to have Brother along, teaching him how to go by himself someday. He was special to the family, because he was the firstborn son. Mother was perpetually having babies, in due time giving birth to nine—five boys and four girls. The teachings of Confucius dated so far back that no one considered where the ideas had come from, but from that ancient time until the present, Oldest Son has held a peculiar place of honor and respect in the East. In Korean thinking, the worst disgrace of any family was to have no boys, but the highest virtue was to have a son.

In old Korea, certain families in the north had sold young daughters in order to have money for food. At an early age the girls became common servants to wealthier families, and some became prostitutes. The higher class families owned many children as long as they were useful.

Since the turn of the century, however, the Japanese had torn down the respected class distinctions of Korean society. Considered lower by the Japanese, all Koreans belonged to one social class—poor. On their own soil the Japanese commoners were also starving and sacrificing everything for the war effort; but even the nobodies gained social status when they came to Korea to work, so far were they above the Koreans.

When Korea had been called a "hermit nation," her social chances had been equal; by study and success in government examinations anyone could rise to eminence, perhaps even to power. Confucian ethics, however, placed greatest value on the scholar and conventional social ranking placed the farmer next, then the engineer or entrepreneur, with the merchant low in the hierarchy. As all teachers in the school, plus the government positions, were replaced by Japanese, Koreans lost all prestige regardless of their ability. Any semblance of rank was determined by who you knew and what favors you could provide them.

Yet from the highest to the lowest, in every social rank of both nationalities, the eldest son would be expected to carry on his father's memory, and especially to perform proper worship of the ancestors, as well as to see to it that he also left sons to do so in the future. The Chinese character which Koreans and Japanese used for filial piety (孝) abstractly placed an old man with a walking stick (耂) on the shoulders of a child (子), graphically indicating that while the parents were alive they were to be supported and respected; and after their death the prescribed sacrifices were to be offered to them.

Any plans or undertakings which the parents may have started were also to be carried out to completion after their death. These were someday to become the duties of Yonggi Cho, the firstborn son. Because of his special position in the Cho household, Older Sister must take unusual care to protect him. Nor was that difficult for her to do, for even in the fourth grade of elementary school she knew her place as a woman was to be lower than Brother's, but there was a certain pride and satisfaction in having a brother to take care of. It was assumed that the gods favored the family, to have blessed them with a boy. From the day he was born, everyone said he would become a special figure when he got to be a man because his face was long and not round and because they saw intelligence in his eyes.

Father had planted trees along the path nearest the house, to grow as a memorial to his firstborn son. In six years the saplings had shot up taller than the boy, a good sign that he too would get the start he needed to succeed and make it as high as he was supposed to go. Any capability he might possess as a man depended on his capacity to grow. Any influence as a teacher or leader of others would be commensurate to his power to sway with the wind yet come back always to a straight and tall position.

The trees stood ever reminding the son of one's utter dependence on the gods in Korea. But for the god of rain, there could be no existence. They must constantly beseech the goddess of mercy, lest all be destroyed by storms or lightning; and be ever thankful to Mother Earth, that goddess of goodness who receives the seed and gives it birth. The glory of Earth is in the life she brings forth, and on the distant hillsides there is no spot so ugly as the barren earth. There was an increasing list of gods, with fear and hunger causing constant reasons to pray.

Not only were the memory trees to teach dependence on the gods, but as their roots took hold to withstand the storms, so was endurance expected to form in the son's nature. In crises, in the turning points of his life, Yonggi was reminded of the trees.

An ancient Korean proverb cautioned, "Do not look up at the tree which you can never climb." Already he had asked Miss Arai to marry him when he grew up; how many years would it take him to understand that proverb and the futility of setting his eyes on something which could never be his?

Yonggi held two more of Father's shortened sayings fixed in his mind. "No root, no leaf," he was told, and this meant that if there was no cause then there could be no effect. "No sap from a dry tree"; this one he had to think about for a while. Anyway, he would hear it again. His father made sure of that.

East Asians did not call one another by name but by position-designating titles, addressing each other as "Uncle," or "Teacher," "Little Brother," "Master," etc. Position was fearfully important and the acceptance of it was not to be questioned. Not only in the family, but in society and business, there was a time to serve and a time to be served. One would know his rank, if not by birth, then by education or lack of it, by success or failure, or by the haves and the have-nots.

It did seem that no one was ever quite at the top. Even the gods vied for power. The Japanese Emperor himself had someone above him to honor, as even he, too, was subject to the rituals of the ancestral sacrifices to the spirits of his father and his famous grandfather, the Emperor Meiji.

Since Japan first took over Korea there had been an introduction of Japanese ways in the name of improvements, although some wondered whether improvement meant annihilation of certain people. An early story told of a foreign dignitary's visit to Korea, traveling by Japanese train from Pusan to Seoul. The train was passing along a high, narrow trestle to cross the Nak-Dong River when it lurched to a sudden halt. The river was forceful that day with violent, boiling spume beneath. A coolie was elbowed into the river, his loaded A-frame strapped to his back. He was struggling desperately for a handhold on the steep and slippery bank when the emergency brake on the train was released and the train jerked onward.

"Hold on!" the foreigner shouted. "Can't you see he'll drown?" It would have taken only a few seconds to scramble down and rescue the man.

The Japanese brakeman pulled the cord again, shoved the foreigner back into his seat and went on. "Why you trouble?" he reasoned. "He only a Korean."[1]

It was simple in Korea to know one's social position: only a Korean.

The Japanese were the haves and the Koreans the have-nots. And that made all the difference. Korea had been formally annexed to the Divine Empire of Japan in 1910. At Eonyang Elementary School in Kyung Nam the children were loaded on trucks and taken to work in the fields where the Japanese lived. The Japanese had chopsticks and spoons; the Koreans had turned theirs in to be converted into bullet casings—for the glory of the empire. The Japanese had rice; the Koreans shipped their rice to Japan—for the glory of the empire. Except for their small survival ration and a tiny thanks offering to the faithful scarecrows that protected the fields, the five sacred grains—rice, soy, wheat, millet and barley—were sent to Tokyo, all for the glory of the empire.

"Father, may I ever see the empire?" Yonggi asked one night.

The elder Cho spat upon the ground! "Speak to your father in Korean, boy!" replied his father in an angry whisper. "They have been calling our surname 'Yoshida' since 1940. You hardly know who you are. You are not Japanese, you know! The day is coming when that paper empire is going to burn, and you are going to return to the Cho that you are. You are Korean! Even the tree that has been cut down to a trunk still has its roots and it will bloom again!"

Both glanced about in fear of being overheard using the forbidden language. Korean was reserved for the hidden room out back, where Yonggi's father dared to gather the neighbors' children after supper and teach them secretly how to read and write *Hangul*, the three-hundred-year-old Korean writing system which Japan was attempting to wipe out in one generation. If Father was ever caught, he would be sent straightway to hard labor in the coal mines or off to have his ankles crushed together and his head removed. They would not bother sending him to prison. The use of the Korean language had been banned since 1938, when Yonggi was just beginning to talk at two years old. Japan had a saying, "The world, one household." Land expansion and assimilation meant, for one thing, enforced use of Japanese only.

At the end of every secret Korean lesson Father instructed his pupils to write a little Japanese, watching their hands to be sure they did not mix up the Korean characters at school the next day. Because this generation had never used Korean, it would be a sure sign for any Japanese teacher to investigate the possibility of an underground school. The children were sworn to secrecy, mostly in fear of their own fathers, and in fear of the graves of their fathers' fathers that lay all over Korea.

Yonggi listened as his father dug a trench behind their house at night, getting ready for the share of rice which he wanted to hold back at harvest time. Except for the fresh smell of dirt, there was not a trace the next morning that anything different had been done in the night. Mats, a tree limb and leaves covered all. This hidden storage bin meant survival to the Cho family, and the Japanese soldiers were to traverse the very spot time and time again, their boots never suspecting the grains of rice concealed below. Like badgers, all families hid their food.

Cho laughed at the Japanese surname he had been given. *Yoshida* meant "lucky rice field." The imperial regime meant it for the prosperity of their own gain, but the "lucky rice field" lay at the back doorsteps for the Korean family that burrowed inside.

Every family name was changed to Japanese. Convince a

man he is somebody else, and his old identity is supposed
to die. Without recognizing that they borrowed an
ancient biblical principle, the Japanese were directing
their subjects to put off the old man and put on the new.
Nor did they know it could not happen by outward
design, lest the inner man remain unchanged. Korean
dress was changed to Japanese. Korea was called *Chosen*
(pronounced "Cho-sen" with a hard *s*), the Japanese
corruption of the nation's historically Chinese name,
Choson, which meant "Land of the Morning Calm."
Seoul was renamed Keijo, Pyongyang became Heijo,
Pusan was Fusan, and other cities, rivers and mountains
were renamed, giving the land a new geography. Korean
history was taken out of the school curriculum altogether.
Korea did not exist. Her newspapers had long been
banned and books were burned.

The very year Yonggi was born, a Korean named Son
Ki Jong won the 1936 Olympic marathon race in Berlin
but was forced to run it for Japan, with the Japanese flag
on his chest. When a Korean newspaper printed his
picture with the Korean flag substituted for the Japanese,
the paper was immediately suspended from publication.

The Japanese colonial system tightened as the war days
wore on, and so did life. School itself was not the place it
once had been, not with growing up and advancing to
Corporal Shigeo Kai's classroom. In snow there was
scraping to do, scraping ice away from Teacher's path
using tree limbs for shovels. One's wet pant legs would
freeze around the ankles. In spring, school was for the
express purpose of glorifying the empire by working
most of the week in the Japanese fields. A little

mathematics, a little Japanese writing, and world history doctored up a bit sufficed to call it school. The teachers being military men, school children saluted them as the customary greeting.

"Yoshida, are you a highly privileged boy to get to attend school in these days of Western barbarism while other children in the world must stay at home and be deprived of an education?" It was part of Corporal Kai's routine.

Yonggi jumped to his feet to address the Sensei. "Yes, Teacher!" came back the quick reply.

"Is that all?" barked the corporal.

Bowing low, his arms stiff on both sides, Yonggi then straightened up to start again. "I'm sorry. It is a rare privilege and I am eternally thankful to the glorious and immortal Empire of Japan. Thank you for permitting my lowliness to stand before one so mighty as the great Kai Sensei and to draw from his knowledge and kindness."

"Straighten out your hands at both sides when you address a gentleman! Uncurl your fingers and look at the lice on the head in front of you until I order you to move!"

This punishment was easier than most, Yonggi thought. Worst of all, he hated being stripped of his clothes and forced to expose himself in the circle of girls and other classmates who were made to watch. Worse yet was if Miss Arai ever caught him in such a predicament. He knew the girls were as embarrassed as he was every time that happened. But no child laughed at a fellow-classmate's tortures; there is something that binds a people who suffer together, and further cruelty only serves to strengthen the bond.

Yonggi had always been careful to bow properly when the portrait of His Imperial Highness, the Emperor, was unveiled for the class to worship. In the daily physical exercises he had likewise taken care to bend low at the waist, for the routine placed all their knee bends and bows facing the direction of Tokyo, the Eastern capital, where the Imperial Palace was located. Even in the bodily movements of a routine exercise drill, one never bent in a direction opposite from Tokyo, as it would be unheard of to display one's buttocks toward the throne of His Majesty. On the soil of Japan, in case the Emperor and Empress or the Crown Prince were riding by on the train or in a limousine, no face of the people dared look upon them. Claimants to the throne had never once seen a common face on their travels other than occasional children who knew no better than to look upon the Emperor. The wooden shutters of windows in the city were closed when the Emperor needed to go by, lest a commoner look upon him from the higher level. Some believed their own eyes would be blinded if they looked at the Emperor. He was the living god of Japan and of every Japanese scattered throughout the Pacific and Asia in this time of conquest for "the world, one household." Soldiers were fighting this war for more than Japan; they fought for their god. And if need be, women, children and the aged would fight for him too.

"Sit down, stupid!" came the schoolboy's release at last. Corporal Kai shouted the order in time for Yonggi's weary legs to trudge up the mountain to his home. Maybe they could catch a couple of nice, juicy locusts and roast them for a snack along the way. Or they could at least use some rocks to chunk down a few half-opened chestnut burrs from a tree and boil the chestnuts when they got home.

A new fear nagged him now. What if suspecting soldiers came and dragged Father away? What if the spies overheard Mama's Korean because she could not speak Japanese very well?

He wondered whether Grandmother would always be waiting for him at the gate or at the edge of the cemetery as she often walked with him the last few meters home. Already he knew his special place in the household, and Grandmother saw to it that her grandson wanted for nothing if she could provide it for him. Grandfather had been an orphan but he had been clever and he used his brain planning and working out wealth through the land. Cho Sung Do dressed his grandchildren in the best and delighted to hear how other children stroked the fabrics and admired their coats. When Yonggi was a baby he had not received the silver chopsticks and spoon in traditional Korean celebration of the one-hundredth-day anniversary, and Grandfather tried to make up for it. On his first birthday he had been dressed in the traditional costume, light blue pants and a peach-colored jacket with the lower half of the sleeves brightly banded in broad red, dark blue and green stripes. Over this coat was the customary dark blue vest with three red buttons down the front, and on his head a special black hat with the Chinese characters for "long life" and "fortune" in gold on the sides, and two black ribbons hanging down the back. In spite of hard times, this first grandson had been seated among piles of rice cakes, cookies, yut candy made of rice, and fruit, and he had been offered a number of gifts. Grandfather had offered him the traditional writing brush and coins, along with pieces of thread (for long life), as it was believed that whichever the infant grasped first predicted the child's future career as a scholar or a businessman. It was the household joke that the baby had grabbed both coin and brush at the same time.

The family gathered after dark for a special conference. No one knew of his punishment at school that day, but there was a tenseness in the air. Usually it was Father who took these matters in hand, but tonight Mama did it. "You know, Children, your humble mother does not have the learning that you are getting. It is not easy for you to make out my poor Japanese words because I was not schooled in them. But we are facing a grave time and we must all act like real Yoshidas. It can't be helped. Our own Korean language has been lawed against, and I fear that these days of war will bring trouble for sure unless we bend to the whip.

"Your humble mother is asking you from this night forward to permit nothing but Japanese words to escape from your lips." A tear slipped away and ran down her apron to hide. "Even when talking with Mama!" she added with a new breath of bravery. Her nose turned red and she continued her speech.

"For two years Father has been graciously causing you to read and write the beautiful Korean *Hangul* language of your heavenly grandfathers, but we have decided to stop the lamplight school due to possible dangers connected with war. Down in the village there is rumor that a mother has been snatched up and taken away from her babies because she was talking Korean. In times like these we must act unitedly for the best of our family. It is only foolish to spit to the sky while lying on our backs.

"So we meet tonight to agree on these measures."

Mama stopped, but all knew she was not finished. Each sat on the *ondol* floor, made of baked clay covered with glazed paper and heated from underneath, though any heat had long since left the room. Eyes stared at the flickering candle as if wondering how much longer it could hold out. All about the room the shadows loomed larger than the light it could cast, yet the tiny flame tried hard. Father picked up the lone chopstick that he had fashioned out of a twig, had peeled the bark away and scrubbed it up, then in the silence he broke it in his hand. No one dared look up, or hardly breathe, till Mama spoke again.

"The soldiers have got restless here of late, drawing their swords at a mosquito. I think there must be more to this war than they let on to us. As long as they are winning somewhere, they leave us alone for a while and things don't seem so bad. You watch it. Sure as their victory news to us is fake, you see their glittering sword whack off a cat's head or a dog's hind parts. Things are happening in the village that make me wonder whether something might be about to happen that is bigger than anything you Children have known so far.

"Eldest Brother, you were born February 14, 1936, only two years and two months behind the Crown Prince, whose bones are growing inside his flesh in Tokyo the same as yours are growing on this hill across the sea. The blood that runs in you is *Cho* Yonggi. But from tonight

16

you will become the best Japanese boy you can possibly be, not only in the words you speak, but also in the thoughts you think. Nor will you speak evil of any teacher or any other who is Japanese. From tonight Korea is forgotten; this is Japan and we are Japanese. My son, you are *Yoshida* Yonggi—at home as well as school. This is the name they forced on us, and now after all these years let us accept it. It can't be helped. There is no other way. If the dreadful day ever comes when you are conscripted to serve in the Imperial Army, you will go and you will serve and you will be the best Japanese soldier that Corporal Kai could ever teach you to be. Do you have anything to say?"

He wished he could hug her tightly and cry. But this was a family consultation, and whether or not he understood it he knew it was serious business. He must try to be as strong as Mama. He hardly remembered seeing her without a baby tied to her back if not a new one swelling her stomach, and the water crock balancing on her head as she carried it up the bank. He did not know why Father would not help her carry those heavy things except he had said certain things were women's work. Yonggi had sat with his mother day after day as she pounded dripping clothes against the rocks to get them clean down at the stream. He had seen the Japanese housewives stirring their pots with shiny spoons and long, slender chopsticks, while his own mother stirred bean paste soup with only a twig. He did have questions, plenty of them.

"Yes, I have one question," Yonggi stared at the candle and addressed his question in Japanese: "Why do we have to go to school?"

Father looked at Mama, and Mama looked at Father. They seemed to have a secret way of knowing whose turn it was.

"No sap from a dry tree," deliberated Father, the movement of his head emphasizing every word, punctuated by the eye-to-eye contact that made it final.

"Hai, wakarimashita!" ("Yes, I understand!") He spoke to Father in clear, polite Japanese, bowing with fingers straightened on his knees.

As for the things Mama had said concerning war, he did not fully understand; nevertheless, it seemed true. He remembered the surrender of a place called Singapore and how the whole school had let out for a parade through the village and new maps were colored in to show the greatness of the Empire. He had seen even Kai Sensei laugh and fly a kite the teacher himself had made to depict the Rising Sun flag of Japan. He had wished the god of rain would send a downpour and soak Kai's kite so that it would not flutter at all. Instead the sun shined and the Japanese were drunk with joy, clapping as if their very own sun goddess, Amaterasu, herself had appeared. The children had been free to use all the bad words they were restricted from using at school to refer to General MacArthur who was burned in effigy that day—all the words schoolchildren could come up with plus others the Japanese soldiers taught them. Oh, that MacArthur guy must have been some kind of real devil.

It seemed lately, though, that there were not many victory marches any more, and that bowing to the photo of his Majesty the Emperor became more frequent.

Families were called on to pray for victory; if they did not have a god in their home to entreat, then they should make one. A church down in the valley was commanded to exhibit the Emperor's photo behind the pulpit, where the people were to bow to him every Sunday, to burn incense before the ancestral shrine, and to pray to the Christian God, not for peace but for victory on behalf of the Divine Empire of Japan. Mama was right. There was a restlessness in the air, all right.

Riding on the truck after working in the fields one afternoon, the schoolchildren saw the church on fire and Yonggi wondered at the Japanese soldiers standing with arms folded, watching the black smoke pour out. The truck stopped and the driver laughed as he pointed to a window on the side of the building. A mother was pushing her baby out the open window, and a soldier ran forward to poke it back into the blaze. A strange combination of moans and singing could be heard as barred doors held the congregation while the fire burned them all to death. Yonggi did not know what that fire had to do with a war that was being fought in remote islands somewhere, but he was glad no one in his family was a Christian.

If Mama's guess was right, then the Imperial Army or Navy must have really suffered a terrible defeat somewhere to cause the church to get burned like that. For what other reason, he could not imagine. He hurried home and looked into the kitchen; Mama was not there. Maybe she was down at the spring.

No, nobody there. Not even a single dragonfly.

He had work to do, and there was no time to look for

Mama. But he could not do his work until he found her.

"Please , please, god of sky, don't let it get dark until I do my work. O god of kitchen, show me where Mama is." Both hands rubbed up and down in constant prayer. "O god of toilet, I'm so sorry if I ever teased you and made you angry. I know that I am supposed to step up right foot first; if I have ever forgotten or if I was in too big a hurry to pay attention, please forgive me if I ever stepped up with my left foot first. I did not mean to insult you. I know I have never spit in your face, O god of toilet, so please be kind and help Mama too, wherever she is. O I thank you, dear god of toilet."

Again he looked in the kitchen. With its sunken dirt floor, the kitchen was dug down about two feet deeper than the level of the ground outside. Maybe Mama was squatting down in the corner to pick up the dry grass and stalks to feed the fire she cooked on. Grandmother kept the babies and Mama did the cooking. Maybe his eyes had not seen her before. As he threw open the door again it startled him to see her standing beside the stove. No, she had not been there before. He tried not to show his relief. She was just standing there shooing flies off a fish head. As his eyes met hers he could tell she had been crying. Her nose was still red. He quickly bowed to her and went outside to do his work, with no word spoken except, *"Tadaima"* (Japanese for "I've returned home"), the common greeting of every family member upon an arrival back home. As he hastened away she turned her head to the wall but returned his greeting with the simple, *"Okaerinasai,"* the Japanese way of acknowledging, "You are happily returned, welcome home."

He guessed she must have been out to a neighbor's house to give them their turn at using the kitchen knife. The Japanese had "disarmed" all Koreans so that one kitchen knife was permissible among every four families.

It had been a long time since they enjoyed fish head soup. Maybe tonight it would have a little rice floating in it too and, oh, to have some fried garlic on the side with a lot of *kimchi. Kimchi* was for every meal, but there never seemed to be more than a mere taste and not enough to eat these days even though the landowning Cho household was said to have more than everyone else. Mama was always adding soaked cucumbers to make it look like more on the table.

But kimchi was special, one of the spiciest foods of the world and no doubt the dish that kept a family healthy. In November, Yonggi had kept the younger children away from the women's work area on kimchi-making day, so that they would not get any hot peppers in their eyes. The mothers and able grandmothers of the four families sharing the common knife carried the large heads of curly-leafed Chinese cabbage to the well. They wilted the cabbage in strong salt water, then washed and washed each head like rags. Some scrubbed the big long white radishes known as *daikon,* while someone else made the hot seasoning mixture. They chopped red peppers, garlic, onions and ginger, and twisted all this together inside each cabbage head. Finally they packed the radishes and cabbages into big earthen jars in alternate layers with salt sprinkled between the layers. Extra radish leaves were put on top and in each jar a big scrubbed rock weighted down the vegetables. The jars were left in the shade or under the ground for the kimchi to pickle and ferment over a long period of time. It normally took about ten gallons of kimchi per person for the winter, but these days they seemed to get no more than a small bite of it. Even so, it helped on cold days. Summer kimchi was different and was often made on a daily basis; there must have been as many kinds of kimchi as there were hills in Korea.

Yonggi met Father at the pine trees. "This one is not going to make it to a full jar, I'm afraid," he pointed to his son's jar of pine sap they had been catching since the night before. If it was not full, Teacher would really storm out at him when he turned it in the next day at school, as each pupil was required to bring a full jar of pine oil every day for greasing the fighter airplanes.

"Father, what is life?"

Father went to the next tree, tore the bark away and cut a deep shape, lifting up the wound and tying the jar so that it would catch the thick ooze as if bleeding from an injury.

"Father, what is the use of living? These bodies can burn away to nothing or bury in the ground and decay like leaves. What are we doing here?"

The smell of burned human flesh lingered over the countryside for days. At night it was in the bedroom, and in the daytime it permeated the air over the fields. Even the wind was too weak to take away the strange smell hovering over the village as the ashes of the church smoldered yet.

"What is life?" he asked again.

"You, small boy, you think too much. Don't pester

me." Father did not care to discuss such a question. He himself had been born under the Japanese flag only three years after the official annexation, but Grandfather had disallowed his own ambitions to develop. He had longed to go to college in Japan but Grandfather said schooling was not necessary—they were rich; why should they have to go to Japan for schooling? Father felt stuck on a piece of land that he hated and he and Mama started having babies when he was twenty. Unplowed fields make hollow bellies, but as far as Father was concerned, unread books made hollow minds. As his son stood before him these eight years a sapling in the image of himself, Father wondered, too, about the meaning of life. In blood they were born and by blood the world was dying; there were wars and rumors of wars.

"It's getting dark, so you'd better hurry and cut out the grass now. Anyway, tonight for sure you will have to get Mama to boil a potato."

When the jar of pine oil did not fill up, potatoes were used. They might not oil an airplane very well, but mashed up and mixed with the tree sap, it all looked the same. The hardest part was when another classmate would sneak up and steal a jar from a tree in the night so that he could turn it in as his own. As soldiers of the Empire it was the children's duty to bring a jar full of pine oil every day to school, along with a square carpet of grass freshly dug as from a lawn.

Cutting out the square of sod every day made blisters on the hand. Father sometimes cut it for both children. Today he did the hardest part but left a corner on both pieces for Yonggi to finish. Every morning this green homework was routinely checked off with the roll call. He did not see how, but these grassy plots were to be used in making runways for the aircraft of war.

There was a time to work and a time to think, a time to eat and a time to talk; but tonight Mama seemed more solemn than before. Yonggi could tell by the way Sister regarded Mama over the edge of her soup bowl that she knew more than he did. Women, he supposed, had secrets between them. He wondered whether Sister would try to bribe him or whether she might tell him freely.

He suspected that being extra nice to her would not help either; she knew that trick. Being over-polite could mean, "I want something."

As expected, Sister was too smart to let it pass. "Wag Baby on your back for three days after school," she demanded. "If Father asks what you are doing, explain to him you want to make friends with Baby Sister, so you carry her on your back for a few days while you dig the grass."

Yonggi hated the trickling of warm urine down his back when the babies did not know any better, but he and Sister locked the little fingers of their right hand together as a pledge, Japanese style. This was called *yubikiri*. In a so-called blood covenant at the first knuckle, the agreement was on! Three days it would be! The cost of news was expensive. It was woman's work to wag babies around.

When the third day came, Sister demurely announced, "I have two bits of news. Which do you wish to hear?"

"Well, how can I answer that question? You please tell

me what is my right to know!"

"Number one, Mama is going to have another baby."

"Why does she want to give us one more baby? Already she has five of us, and two are boys. Why another baby? But I wonder, can Mama tell me what is life, then? I saw that baby burn up in the church window, and I just want to know where it came from and where it went to. Now just a few days after that baby disappeared, Mama can go and find another one?"

"Brother, don't you want to hear one more bit of news?"

"Mama was crying in the kitchen that day. What for?"

"Maybe she cried for both. Anyway, the soldiers came and they snatched away the wedding ring that Father had put on her finger a long time ago. They said they have to take all the temple bells and the wedding rings, so they can make a lot of bullets. Took the boiling kettle, too, and the fry pan. She cooks everything now in the wooden steam stove. In the village they took the water pipes too."

Sister talked on about wedding rings and circles that get broken and circles that never end but keep going on forever. Yonggi wondered what a bullet looked like.

Mainly he wondered what a barbarian looked like. Could those Americans really be as tall as bamboo trees? Teacher had told them the Americans had noses that stuck out so far they had to really stretch their arms to wash them.

School had taken on a new sport lately. The pupils were learning how to thrust a spear sharpened out of bamboo. Since the barbarians were so tall, the "Children of Valor" were practicing how to thrust a spear as if through enemy legs and then run up and bite the leg off. That was the only way. That, and one other way. The children were

25

trained to roll under an army tank holding a grenade in their hands. Only the Korean children.

Bravery was a great virtue; and the tougher the giant, the higher the glory.

The rains flooded the river during the spring of third grade, and the boys stood on the banks and dared one another to swim in the rapid current. Yonggi could not stand himself for his cowardly prayers every afternoon before running through the cemetery. He would never tell his friends how scared he was to walk home through those dark, squatting trees standing there looking as if at any moment they would cry out and spring at him. Now here was his chance to beat the other fellows. While everybody watched, he stepped forward with his chest out: "Okay, here's your man!" he said of himself. "I'll swim it!"

"Ha! This little puppy is too young to fear the tiger!" spurned an older boy.

Seeing only a waiting audience that would make him great, Yonggi thrust his shoulders back, turned quickly and jumped into the raging waters below.

Unable to maneuver under the onslaught of rushing water, his body was thrown from side to side, knocked about as if he were a first-time wrestler. In moments he was washed mercilessly downstream like debris, with the angry river god furiously beating him as he cowered. Landing bruised and bleeding upon a rock, he cried as if by instinct, "O unknown God, save me!" The waters picked him up again and slapped him in the face. Something slowed their course and he gained his swimmer's stance. Blindly he clawed at the river, bluffing for survival as he kicked his way back upstream.

He found his way to a muddy bank and grasped hold of the twisted, twining roots of a tree. *"Banzai! Banzai!"* ("Victory, Victory!") Over his own heavy breathing he heard classmates running toward him. He would not open his eyes yet. It felt good to be alive—and he could do without their humiliating jeers; he knew he had attempted a stupid thing and he must have really looked stupid bouncing around like that, yelling and screaming.

"The great Yoshida, Number One!" There it came again. They were making fun of him. Oh, why could he not have died down in the flooded river, after all? He felt too exhausted to fight back. One of the fifth-grade boys climbed down the bank and took Yonggi's arms to lift him up. "Hey, Yoshida, I didn't know you had it in you. You know what? We're all going to make you president of the student body. Just like your name 'Yonggi' means in Korean, you're the brave one, all right! You did all right, man! Now, can you make it up to the field?"

Yonggi looked around. They were not joking. He had become a hero. He stood to his feet, but it was good to feel the fifth grader give him a boost up the bank. "He's bleeding. Who's got the cleanest handkerchief?" his new friend demanded.

He hoped they would not wipe it all off yet, feeling braver as long as there was blood. It seemed the honor might go away if there was not a scar to show for it.

The new hero got home in time to cut out his square of grass, and was glad to find Father still in the peach orchard propping up the limbs after the heavy rain. In the darkness it was good no one noticed his bruises, so he would not have to make up some tale more fitting for home sympathy. Even the valiant often have to go without honor among their own kindred.

He wished he knew what kind of root it was that Mama used to mash into the white of an egg and lay on a bruise or a swelling. But his parents must never find out about that river stunt. How much of a man's life, he wondered, was kept secret from at least someone. Only Sister knew the number of times he had kowtowed to the gods, frightened to numbness by the sudden appearance of a fox or the screech of an eagle. He wondered whether other boys in his class were afraid to get up in the night to go to the bathroom—did they too have to walk past a shadowy old chicken coop and imagine all sorts of devils in the wispy shapes? He hoped no one had heard him cry out to that unknown God to save him from drowning in the river. Now that he was big man at school, he would certainly like to forget such a moment. It severed him from all reality. Such despair. Such weakness. No, he would never tell anyone he had cried out to an unknown God.

In the weeks ahead a turn of events started which stirred up the Koreans and infuriated the Japanese. Leaflets were found in open fields, along the paths to school, in the villages, everywhere. Printed in the forbidden Korean language, the papers had apparently been dropped from above. But what enemy airplane could carry such friendly warnings, even if such a plane possibly existed?

Attention, dear Korean people: Koreans are instructed to please wear white clothing. . . .

The leaflets were printed in *Hangul* on top, and English on the lower half.

. . . white clothing. If we are obliged to drop further bombs of fire on the Japanese ammunitions plants to expedite a peaceful settlement to the war, it is not our aim to destroy innocent human lives, but to cause the people to appeal to their government to stop the war. Korean people, wear white to facilitate identification. Help will come for you soon.[2]

The traditional white clothing had been strictly forbidden, and now there was going to be absolute surveillance. What would happen if Father put on white bloomer trousers now? Surely the Japanese soldiers would come wielding the sword before any bombs had time to strike. Would any Japanese dare to put on the Korean whites in order to deceive an airborne enemy? Or would they rather die than stoop to the lower man's clothing?

It was the summer of 1945, known in Korea as the Japanese year *"Showa* 20," the twentieth year under the reign of Emperor Hirohito of Japan. This period was known as "The Era of Enlightenment and Peace," a misnomer for all times. (The present *Tenno Heika* [His Majesty the Emperor] had come to the throne on Christmas Day, 1926.) No one was allowed to call the Emperor by his name nor did anyone consider whether he had a name, as it was too sacred to utter. The youth of Korea were caught in the middle—neither Japanese nor Korean, yet a little of both. When the Japanese were winning, the victory sometimes seemed their own and they were proud. Yet when the Japanese met defeat, they were at the same time both glad and sorry. Ambivalent as to whose war this was, they had been born as Japanese children of the

Empire while their fathers held pure Korean hatred for anything Japanese, a hatred inherited and seasoned with gall in the next generation.

From the schoolyard this in-between generation looked up and in total surprise saw that the airplane overhead was not marked by the Rising Sun flag. Chill bumps darted up Yonggi's neck as more leaflets streamed to earth, shimmering like manna in the cloudless sky. Children feigned ignorance and inability to read the Korean-written message, holding the leaflets upside-down if Teacher was anywhere in sight.

"Wow! What a fantastic, glittering plane!" Yonggi said, gesturing to show the graceful movements of the white, silvery plane with his hands as all boys do. From under his breath there slipped the real question in his mind: "If those Americans are barbarians, how come they can create such a shiny plane able to come all this way to where we live in Korea? If they are so barbaric and stupid, how come the Japanese planes did not stop them before they got this far?"

The plane was still a spectacle in the sky when Teacher barked out to the students, "Okay, stupid Children of Valor, line up and march yourselves into the room—on the double!" That Kai Teacher was always a corporal, for sure.

"And you, Yoshida. Come to the front of Teacher's desk and stand where everybody can see you.

"All right, everybody, I want you to get a good look at your river hero!" No one giggled. No one spoke. No one whispered nor hardly breathed. All cringed.

With one blow of Kai's backhand, Yonggi fell to the

wooden floor, his lip bleeding into his mouth where he lay; and in full force the teacher jumped on the boy's stomach. He jumped again. And again. Bracing against the desk, the man positioned his boots and stood on Yoshida, to lecture the class. "Take your hands from off your stomachs, every last one of you. Quit crumpling up as if it were yourself on the floor! Sit up straight and put both hands on top of your desk!"

Picking up one leg, Kai heeled his boot into the stomach he stood upon.

"You must all learn a lesson from the foul language used by fool Yoshida outside a few minutes ago!" Saliva drooled from the corporal's mouth as he spoke, his eyes set with intensity. "You have heard a lot of stories about what happens to traitors to the Divine Empire. Children of Valor, you are looking at a *traitor!*" he bellowed as he pointed to Yonggi writhing on the floor, trying desperately to breathe. On the boy's face came that frightful look of bugged eyes and a red forehead, the scariest moment of a person's life—unable to breathe, he turned his head every direction gasping, flinging his arms for one more breath, and none would come.

Kai jumped off and laughed loudly, stomped to the window with his arms folded across his chest and guffawed in hysterics.

2

Korea Is Born Again

(1942-1945)

The first breath came back in the form of a short gasp. The next was choppy and faltering. Grappling for life, the boy on the schoolroom floor clutched with awkward fingers for air. He got another partial breath, and another. At last an uncertain pulsation was seen in his chest and spasmodic sounds of life brought a sigh from the classmates who sat immovable with their fists clenched on the tops of their desks.

"Oh, ho! The worm wriggles again!" yelled the corporal. Kai stalked back to the fitful figure, squatted on his haunches and gritted out a message: "You need a bath!" He spat virulently, squarely into the boy's face—not once, but three times, then he stood with his hands on his hips and stomped out of the building.

The war was over.

Freedom came to the Korean nation on August 15, 1945; the traditional way of reckoning was restored to the year 4278 in honor of Tangun, the nation's legendary founder. School-boys hugged and jumped and jumped and hugged.

The village women ran about embracing the first persons they saw. Men wept and laughed and threw their hats in the air for joy.

For thirty-six years Korea had chafed under the Japanese boot. Like a boy gasping for breath, the entire nation breathed convulsively with intermittent fears that the boot might pounce again, or that the breath which was breathed today might be the last.

It was at noon on August 15 that the Emperor spoke on radio.[3] Conjectured to be a descendant of the sun goddess, Amaterasu, the head of state broadcast his message at the moment when the sun stood at its highest peak, neither setting nor rising, Wednesday noon, the middle of the day and the middle of the week. Hardly could the common man grasp such formal language of the court even in Japan; but wherever the voice was heard, listeners rose to their feet and bowed and remained standing beside the radio for the duration of his speech. A voice of the Japanese god was being heard:

> To our good and loyal subjects: After pondering deeply the general trends of the world and the actual conditions obtaining in our Empire today, we have decided to effect a settlement of the present situation by resorting to an extraordinary measure.
>
> We have ordered our Government to communicate to the Governments of the United States, Great Britain, China and the Soviet Union that our Empire accepts the provisions of their joint declaration.
>
> To strive for the common prosperity and happiness of all nations as well as the security and well-

being of our subjects is the solemn obligation which has been handed down by Our Imperial Ancestors and we lay it close to the heart.

Indeed, we declared war on America and Britain out of our sincere desire to ensure Japan's self-preservation and the stabilization of East Asia, it being far from our thought either to infringe upon the sovereignty of other nations or to embark upon territorial aggrandizement.

But now the war has lasted for nearly four years. Despite the best that has been done by everyone— the gallant fighting of the military and naval forces, the diligence and assiduity of our servants of the State and the devoted service of our one hundred million people—the war situation has developed not necessarily to Japan's advantage, while the general trends of the world have all turned against her interest.

Moreover, the enemy has begun to employ a new and most cruel bomb, the power of which to do damage is, indeed, incalculable, taking the toll of many innocent lives. Should we continue to fight, it would not only result in an ultimate collapse and obliteration of the Japanese nation, but also it would lead to the total extinction of human civilization.

Such being the case, how are we to save the millions of our subjects, or to atone ourselves before the hallowed spirits of our imperial ancestors? This is the reason why we have ordered the acceptance of the provisions of the joint declaration of the powers.

We cannot but express the deepest sense of regret to our allied nations of East Asia, who have consistently co-operated with the Empire towards the emancipation of East Asia.

The thoughts of those officers and men as well as others who have fallen in the fields of battle, those who died at their posts of duty, and those who met with death and all their bereaved families, pains our heart night and day.

The welfare of the wounded and the war sufferers, and of those who have lost their home and livelihood is the object of our profound solicitude. The hardships and sufferings to which our nation is to be subjected hereafter will be certainly great.

We are keenly aware of the inmost feelings of all you, our subjects. However, it is according to the dictates of time and fate that we have resolved to pave the way for a grand peace for all the generations to come by enduring the unendurable and suffering what is unsufferable. Having been able to save and maintain the structure of the Imperial State, we are always with you, our good and loyal subjects, relying upon your sincerity and integrity.

Beware most strictly of any outbursts of emotion that may engender needless complications, and of any fraternal contention and strife that may create confusion, lead you astray and cause you to lose the confidence of the world.

Let the entire nation continue as one family from generation to generation, ever firm in its faith in the imperishableness of its divine land, and mindful of its heavy burden of responsibilities, and the long road before it. Unite your total strength to be devoted to the construction for the future. Cultivate the ways of rectitude, nobility of spirit, and work with resolution so that you may enhance the innate glory of the Imperial State and keep pace with the progress of the world.[4]

To the Japanese it was a blow which they were unable to accept and thousands committed suicide. A lot of Koreans were not sure what it meant, nor were they prepared at all to be a nation. Police and politics had been in the hands of the Japanese, and all underground leadership was yet in exile somewhere in China or some other far-off Narnia. However, soon Keijo was renamed "Seoul," and Korean radio greetings began to pour in. *"Anyong haseiyo!"* ("Be in peace! Be in peace!") It was the everyday expression like "Hello" which had been silenced for so long. A more beautiful word never sounded on the ears of man. *"Anyong hashimnika."* No one but a lonely Jewish tribe uttering *"Shalom"* might feel a kindred spirit and comprehend the depths of the Korean heart this day. "Peace. *Anyong haseiyo, Anyong haseiyo."* Families spoke it over and over. Babies had never heard the sound, yet they paddled feet and hands with excited glee to look into their mother's face as she voiced that word. Aunts and uncles cried when they said it. *"Anyong haseiyo. Anyong hasumnika."*

Russians had come from the north, having declared war on Japan just seven days before the war was ended, and Americans were coming into the south, in order to effect the withdrawal of all Japanese troops at an arbitrarily agreed-upon middle point, the thirty-eighth parallel.

But what promise was there that these powers would not be worse than the former oppressor?

The pulse beat strong as Korean blood was pumped through every artery. *"Anyong haseiyo!* Be in peace, be in peace!"

American jeeps bumped along the village road, honking chickens out of the way as they sped. Children hid behind trees or at the sides of their houses, peeking out to get a glimpse of the long noses they had heard about. "If they are as tall as a bamboo tree, how in the world could they fold their legs into such a jeep?" The schoolboys discussed it among themselves.

As the white flag, with its red and blue monad, crept proudly up the school flag staff, an explosion of noises burst from the crowd of villagers, releasing all that was pent up within them. There it waved, their own flag, her four corners reaching out to the four compass points of the earth as if to announce to the world, "I am!" The circle in the middle symbolized the restoration of balance in all things. It was a banner to pre-established harmony, the red curving into the blue.

For thirty-six years red had dominated as the blood red symbol of Japan had towered over the nation with its rays reaching out like claws in every direction. Sixteen rays waved on the Japanese wartime flag the same as the sixteen petals of the Emperor's chrysanthemum seal. From today, no more.

Dominance and recession, poverty and plenty, war and peace, autumn and spring, seedtime and harvest, male and female—in all things there was balance. Hence the awfulness of yesterday was in fact a promise for tomorrow.

If there was bad, then harmony equaled bad plus good. Korea was becoming a people again. And it was good.

The school building was empty, but it had a flag pole—and around it the village would begin again. A nation with no textbooks was no less a nation, for the seeds are produced from inside; and even the enemy could not steal the seeds which lay dormant far beneath the topsoil.

The Korean flag had been burned, yet it had been resurrected from the ashes of the nation. When neighbors had joined to burn the flag by Japanese edict, old men had folded one here and there into the mud walls of their homes. Today was a day for digging out the hidden treasures where they had been carefully wrapped and plastered into the walls of mud and grass. A few books of poetry, an occasional Bible, the flag, and now and then a stray copy of the Three-One Declaration of Independence of 1919, had been carefully sealed into the sides of a house. More carefully had they been hidden than they were dug out this day, leaving gaping scars in the walls they came from, houses crumbling at the corners, the roof green with fungus giving out a strong earthy smell. The grass and mud had done well, bearing the birth of a nation inside the belly of her homes. Proudly the Caesarean sections were opened and the cries of new breath were heard. Proudly the grass of this generation would be mixed with the earth and water to rebuild her walls. From dust they had come and back to dust they had returned. From dust they would come again.

In four thousand years of history, Korea had built her walls around family clans and they had crumbled. One of the world's oldest civilizations had grown up along the banks of the Yalu River and came to be known as China. Centuries later, in 193 B.C., a Chinese warrior named Wiman crossed that river and conquered the kingdom allegedly founded by a former combatant from China known as Kija. Wiman established a strong government at Pyongyang but his grandson, Ugu, had not been able to hold out against the Chinese armies that attacked in 108 B.C. After defeating Ugu, the Chinese divided northern Korea into four colonies.

Meanwhile, southern Korea was outside of Chinese control, though highly influenced by the culture of that civilization. In 57 B.C., the Koreans in the southeastern part of the peninsula established the kingdom of Silla. The second powerful kingdom, called Koguryo, was formed in 37 B.C. in northern Korea where the Chinese were by then growing weak. A third kingdom, Paekche in southwest Korea, was established in 18 B.C. During the 700 years that followed, the Three Kingdoms fought each other constantly. Walls were built around whole villages, and walls within walls were constructed so that great men's houses lay deep within and far from intrusion. Even so, these crumbled when Silla conquered the other two kingdoms and unified the peninsula.

Because the Silla rulers of Korea remained on good terms with China, the country enjoyed peace. Art, literature, and science flourished. Korea was not in rags but in velvet. Theirs was one of the highest cultures known to man. They spoke a unified language.

Silla kings ruled Korea until 935. Then Wang Kon, a powerful general, overthrew the Silla monarch and re-named the kingdom Koryo, from which the English name

Korea came.

In 1231 Koryo was invaded by tribesmen from Mongolia, and nothing could wall them in or out. The mighty Kubla Khan, the grandson of Genghis Khan, had struck. Many Koreans fled to the offshore islands where the Mongols could not follow, for they had been men of the interior and had no boats. The Mongols occupied the peninsula for sixty years but were finally driven from the nation by General Yi Taejo, who established his own dynasty in 1392.

Korea was called Choson, meaning "Land of the Morning Calm," a name which had been given to this land of mountains and mist in her early history about the time of King David in Israel, a thousand years before Christ. Hanyang, the present city of Seoul, became the capital. The Yi Dynasty governed Choson for almost six hundred years, though not without bloodshed both from within and without. By 1234, two hundred years ahead of Johann Gutenberg's invention of his printing press, Koreans were printing with movable metal type. (A 1377 printing of the Buddhist scriptures is preserved in Paris, France.) The Yi Dynasty saw great leaps in literature, medicine, astronomy, geology, history and agriculture. For the first time in the East, it was possible for the common man to learn to write, as Korean scholars developed the Hangul alphabet, originally twenty-eight characters, later simplified to the present twenty-four, the language system which has remained one of the great wonders of writing simplicity worldwide. Both the Chinese ideographs and the Korean characters were used simultaneously then as now. Some men scorned the simplification and rebuked it as the downfall of the kingdom because now even the lowly woman would be able to read and the scholar's position would thereby be threatened, if not his own dignity destroyed.

Bordered on the northeast by Russia, the west by Manchuria, and just 120 miles across the sea by Japan, Korea almost constantly has been another Israel on her side of the globe. For some reason, every neighbor has wanted her as though she is a perpetual temptation and delicacy hanging down like a ripe cluster of grapes.

The Russians saw her as a gateway to the sea, the Soviet Union having no ice-free harbors eastward. To China she was the outer wall for defense. For the Japanese she was at once a steppingstone to be used in their war with China in 1894-1895, and again in the Russo-Japanese War of 1904-1905, as well as a refuge from earthquakes and a source of food supply and minerals for an ever-increasing population. Indeed, she has been everything to everyone, and the Republic of Korea did not have her own flag until 1882. And this flag had not had the freedom to be exhibited for one full generation. From today it would be different!

Almost four decades since a Korean family had enjoyed the fruits of their own labors, World War II ended just before harvest time. There was hardly anyone alive who remembered having had the land to themselves. Prior to the Japanese order of 1907 to disband the Korean Army, Korea had been prey to China, Russia and Japan for twenty-five years of constant upheaval and her own illustrious Queen Min had been assassinated in 1894. Yet the land was theirs, and neither drought nor famine had separated them from it. Their children's children would bend their backs to the sun, and fill their cups in the morning. They had crawled like bugs between the rows of cabbage, only to give the best to their oppressors. From today the rice also would yield her increase, and the bread of Korea was again going to be her own. The same earth that had formed the homes of their fathers' fathers and the great graveside mounds of their kings would continue to form their homes and feed their babies and mold their gods.

The Cho household resumed the name of Cho. Now if addressed by the former Japanese name, Yoshida, they would jokingly hold out a hand for money the same as they had done before if even one Korean word was ever heard. "*Bachi*! Give me money!"

The entire family went again to the temple, this time not to plead for freedom but to give a thanks offering from the first fruits of the pear trees. They did not wish to offer the usual oranges, as this fruit was brought from Japan at that time, even though the sound of "bitter orange" (*daidai*) contained a double meaning expressing "generation to generation" or longevity. They could never keep the tranquil face that the clay statue of Buddha held before them; in peace or in war, the Buddha remained steadfastly sober, never joyful nor depressed, always the epitome of repose.

They had been fortunate to remain as a family. Hundreds of Korean men in their twenties had been whipped and coerced to marry Japanese girls. Men who finished trade school at twenty-one were told to marry a twenty-year-old girl who had been brought from Japan for the purpose of assimilating the races. If they refused, they were positioned to hold on to a chair while the calves of their legs were beaten along with their backs and shoulders until they relented. Nevertheless, whenever a marriage was consummated, the couple became as one and they could love, in sickness and in health. The cry of each newborn baby had sounded beautiful to either parent and the child's first smile, first faltering steps—all went into making him their own. But history had turned a new page and from the next chapter the Japanese took wives and children back to Japan. Young fathers were torn between hopes for a new Korea and longing for the touch of their own sons and daughters whom they would never see again, sons who might be told of a heroic Japanese father dying in action, never knowing the man in Korea who might be their daddy. Many a face of a Korean man would be painted even by artists for its depth of expression in loneliness and a misty faraway look in the eyes, and the world would not know why and no one would understand.

"Dear Buddha, by your honorable example you have kept our family together all these many years of trouble. It is a comfort to come to this place and be reminded that these things we pass through are as nothing in the great river of time which continues to flow and make us only a tiny rice grain in the colossal past and one with the future. Now, we are about to embark on a new year—no, not new by the calendar, but new for the Cho clan and for all of Korea. We entreat your blessings, along with the blessings of all our deities. Grant us peace, health, and prosperity. Amen."

Yonggi would like to have added, "And protect us from

those awful-looking monsters at the temple entrance."
Two ominous statues with scowling faces, distorted eyes
and threatening pose stood inside the red gate. They
represented mythological kings who guarded all temples
from evil, and were as nightmarish as the cemetery when
the witch woman was there. The incense smelled the
same as hers, only the temple exuded more of it.

The temple bell was conspicuously missing, having been
martyred for the cause of making bullets. The name
"Yonggi" in the Chinese characters was written as a bell
tower or foundation for the iron bell, or drum. Though in
Korean pronunciation it was the same as "courage,"
written in Chinese it implied "one who rings the iron
bell." He wondered what his name had to do with temple
bells or drums and all the frightful things that related to this
god. In Korea it was true that a child's name was prophetic.
The only other bell ringers Yonggi knew were the school-
teacher or the dinner bell caller. Other bells were somehow connected with a curfew of some sort or drums were
connected with some kind of announcement. What in the
world had his father been thinking when he named his
firstborn son "the bell ringer," the drummer?

Chinese	Korean
趙 鏞 基	조용기

As Eonyang was on the direct route to the southern
port at Pusan, retreating Japanese soldiers were constantly passing through. One day they stopped over,
seemingly to give one last scare to the peasants. "Those
Americans are barbaric and totally uncivilized, we're

warning you!" The Japanese jumped out of their trucks to have a smoke and act friendly. Then each one headed for the roadside bushes to perform an act of self-service appropriate to a latrine.

"Be nice. Don't spit. It's nearly over," wives and mothers warned as the men folk gathered cautiously around the trucks. Yonggi stayed close to Mama; in case Kai was ever one of those men out there, he was too afraid of what the corporal might do even yet. The men squatted while they waited, and the women and children listened. It would have been customary to serve tea or among the older men to pass around a smoking pipe when visitors came. But this visit was too close on the heels of havoc to do either. Anyway, swords yet swung from their belts and pistols toyed with leaves as the soldiers looked for targets among the ripening persimmons that spattered like blood when hit.

In the interval between defeat and an effectual withdrawal, the Japanese hacked down whatever trees they could, leaving them to lie by the thousands wherever they fell. "They were planted by Japan," they claimed, as if because they had been unable to destroy a people then at least they could make it hard on birds and other wildlife of the forests. To the Koreans, this final blow was the ultimate insult.

"Yes, for sure you are going to be in a pitiful mess. You're going to have a hard time trying to civilize those American dummies. There is absolutely nothing they know how to do except blunder around and ruin your women. Too bad. The only civilized countries in the world are three—Japan, Germany and Italy."

Just at that moment a bursting noise exploded in the air. An American fighter plane had caught fire and was headed straight for the hill next to the Cho peach orchard. In seconds the pilot bailed out, and as his parachute opened the Japanese soldiers clapped and roared. Pistols were cocked and made ready to fire when he would drift closer.

The new target landed in a tree too far out of range. "Oh, he's not Barabbas—let him hang there and rot!" remarked one who was overheard.

The children ran toward the barbarian hanging in the tree. They had never seen one up close—he had probably got stuck by his nose. In surprise to the schoolboys, Yonggi's father came fast to the scene, got a few other dads to help, and rescued the stranger. In even greater surprise, he looked like any other human being. Except for two things—his eyes were blue and his hair was reddish blond. They guessed he had come from so far up in the sky that his eyes were just sick for a little while. A sixth grader said that all people's eyes would turn blue if they were that high up in the sky very long. The plane had crashed over on the other hill and it was blazing and crackling even yet; everybody agreed that the fire must have done something to turn his hair this strange color. Either that, or it was something he ate.

Yonggi's father, being the only village man who had graduated from high school, knew a few English words. He would try to help that man. First the men took him inside and Father bowed to him, not in the Japanese low waist-style bow but the head and torso slightly bent. Quickly the pilot pulled out a pistol, wishing he could tell the difference between the two races, one an ally the other an enemy. As he looked around, Father surmised that with so many gathered to watch, the newcomer must be afraid he was in for a lynching.

"No. No shoot! Me Korean. You American. Me Korean. You friend."

Quickly handing him pencil and paper, Father motioned as he spoke again, "My name Cho. My name? My name?" As he kept pecking on the paper and pointing to the nose of the guest when he formed his question, Father got across some meaning and the pilot wrote one word: "G-e-o-r-g-e."

The next move was to get him some food. Scratching his head to remember the English word for "chicken soup," Father asked him, "Kitchen water? Kitchen water?" "Kitchen" and "chicken" sounded a lot alike when one never used either.

Another frown as if it were something dirty, and a look of distrust came across George's face and he did not put down the pistol yet. Reasoning that he must have made a mistake, Father remembered one more English word: "Honey water? Honey water?"

George nodded his head yes and Father instructed Mama to mix honey in some water for the visitor to drink. Father drank some too, as a gesture of etiquette. The two men drank in silence, each eyeing the other as if the effects of hemlock might set in momentarily. When the communion was over at last, the pistol was put aside and the two men faced one another as friends. George drew a picture of his airplane on the paper, pointed to the wing, and pulled up his shirt. Half of one side was black, and excruciating pain wrinkled the man's face while he breathed heavily and spasmodically, beading up with perspiration. One kidney area and more had been badly bruised, apparently where his body had not cleared the wing of the wreckage in midair. He needed medical help but there was nowhere in Eonyang to take him.

A day's ride by the three-wheel cart could get him down to where an American camp was setting up, but they would have to pass through the Japanese camp along the way. Cinders still smoldered from the recent defeat, so that the least flare-up might cause ruthless destruction. Nevertheless, George was made ready to travel, and procedures were explained in crude drawings on the paper that said "George." Hay was pitched in the cart for the foreigner's bed, and on top of him as much hay as the cart could hold. A few children were perched on top of the load for innocence, and away they drove, Father out to save the first American they had ever set eyes on. Yonggi was not allowed to go. A firstborn son had responsibilities toward his family, and his first duty was to take heed not to risk unnecessary danger to himself.

The camouflage made it through both lines, and months later Father received a special citation of bravery and honor signed by Lt. General John R. Hodge, Commander, U.S. Military Government in Korea (1945-1948). Mama nagged because Father had not accepted the parachute when George offered it to him as a present; she needed sewing material of any kind, but especially with parachute cloth she could have made clothes that would last a long time.

Life seemed always to have its cycles—exciting and dull, pleasant and sad, busy and boring. Even the dogs and cats appeared to know it. More times than he could remember, the dogs would dig up an old grave and drag a baby's skull to the back yard. Yonggi stared at those sunken temples and hollowed holes where eyes once had been. In a day or two, as if the dogs had known ahead, there would be another funeral procession. He stood on the hillside to watch, but he could never figure out what happened to the real person inside those bodies.

One man had been living on leprosy mountain, where no one ever dared to go, on the other side of the stream that ran behind the Cho land; and a woman had had something else that was supposed to be dreadfully contagious. As all who died of infectious diseases, their bodies were set on fire like animals that died of anthrax.

From everywhere near the cemetery the voices rang out, "Come out, come out, your house is on fire." The sorceress cupped hands around her mouth to call the man's name louder and chanted out to him while his body was burning, "Come out—" Yonggi got as close as he dared, and he could never see any life coming out or going in. What is it? Where does it come from? Where does it go? He could never find out the answers. He had to get back to the peaches and keep the birds shooed away.

If it was not the birds, it was other boys who would come and steal the peaches. He had to always stand watch. Had George Washington really worked at such a dirty job for his father? He was beginning to hate those peaches the same as he had hated Kai. He would be glad when Brother was old enough to watch the peaches.

But that seemed a long way off. Brother got the whooping cough the following winter and at times it seemed he would never get his breath. Mama mixed lard with some roasted onions and rubbed it on his chest. After supper she jerked him up from the floor and beat on his back, somehow beating air back into him. But tonight it would not last very long; his face turned black as if something was strangling him. Someone had to watch him constantly, as every hour he went into a fit of coughing and then sucking noisily for air. Even honey and vinegar would not loosen the croup from Brother's throat. Vomiting had made him weak and, though only a baby, he seemed at times to give up any desire to live; at other times he kicked violently for one more chance.

Yonggi ran to the bedroom and brushed his hands swiftly in a begging prayer to the Japanese god shelf he had kept. Bowing before the *kamidana*, he whispered loudly, this time in Japanese, for Korean did not seem quite proper before a Shinto altar: "Gods, please let my little brother live." He ran back to his brother, and another gasp of air got him through a few more minutes. Father talked of lethargy and pneumonia; Yonggi talked to his brother and told him to fight.

Another coughing spell came right on top of the one just ended and no breath would come. At last, after a long silence, Father took the lifeless body from Mama and she started to shake as big tears streamed down her face. Father laid the body on the floor and asked Mama for a blanket to wrap it in. Yonggi dashed back to the bedroom and bowed again, springing up and down in haste. With clenched fists he demanded in loud Korean, "God above all the gods, will you please make my brother live!" Without stopping for permission he flung himself back to

Brother and lay upon him, pressing mouth to mouth and breathing into the boy on the floor. Yong Mok breathed again. And he kept on breathing until morning, and everyone knew he was going to be all right. What sickness is there to which morning does not bring a promise of change?

The *kamidana* or "god shelf," was supposed to be up high, suspended between the top of the bedding closet and the ceiling. Even if he could not get anyone to help him, Yonggi would at least honor the shelf by dusting it off and putting it as high as he could reach. Among the traditional temples scattered in the mountains, the more important temples were situated at a higher level in the groves. Wherever the Japanese temples had been built on a hillside, the Korean temples were torn down if they were at a higher elevation. It was disrespectful for anything Korean to be higher than Japanese. Had the miniature Shinto altar not been Japanese, he would have liked it better; even so, he would keep it—just in case. Sister complained because it took up space; in daytime the room was for sitting, at nighttime the thin mats were rolled out and the family slept where they had eaten. Paper doors slid along the middle to make the rooms smaller for winter.

Today he would wipe off the white paper hangings in the kamidana or make some new ones. He forgot what they were for—something about the Emperor's white hand of purity reaching out to bless the land with rice and plenty. It had been easy for Yonggi to make the god shelf in the first place, as there was no ugly image in the Shinto style. Mainly a twisted rope draped over the top to mean it closed off the dark tunnel of the past so there could be no looking back. The spirits themselves liked to come here and live.

If he had rice, he would offer it as thanks that Brother had survived. "Shinto" meant "the way of the gods," so he would try to get a cup of rice at least to offer them for coming his way last night. He would save out some of his own breakfast rice if necessary and find an orange-ripe persimmon to please the gods.

The winter snow kept the whole family in drippy colds, but there was plenty of garlic now and that would ward off the flu. Father always knew right where to dig for the ginseng tea roots too. As long as he had gathered in the honey from the hives and there was ginseng, they surely would make it until spring; and pine nuts added to their enjoyment. Mama tried to keep Father in health with a taste of plum wine or peach brandy she managed to squeeze out and keep in hiding until the right timing. Mama was good at hiding things. Even the bean paste and soy sauce never ran out, and she had had a secret place for hiding peach money from the Japanese soldiers. Yonggi wondered whether it might still be under that same crock that looked cracked and useless. He would never have the courage to snoop into Mama's doings nor even to ask what was not his business to know. It was merely paper now anyway, as the currency changed and Korean money was printed.

A few more weeks and the swallows would fly overhead. He liked the swallows better than anything in the world, as they were a sure sign of spring—the swallows and the yellow dust that drifted in from Mongolia. Mama said the plum tree brought the first blossoms of fragrance after the cold and that people should all make their personality like that, welcoming and desirable.

In winter she took the pine bow and told her daughters, no matter how small, that they were to be just like those pine needles, which always grow two-by-two, to someday get married and always work two-by-two, side-by-side with their husbands, enduring stormy hardships and biting cold. She said that was why the pine tree could grow up to be so beautiful, because the pine needles were always evenly matched, two at the base, never changing pattern, even when the tree was old and bent by the wind like the aged women bent by years of sweeping with short-handled brooms.

And one more tree, she said, was in Korea to show the people how to be honest and courageous and bold. Her children's character she wanted to be as straight and tall as the bamboo tree, never having to stoop because of telling a lie or cheating a friend. Be tall and straight, so the one next to you can also grow up straight and tall, she said as she pointed to the bamboo thicket out back. The plum, the pine and the bamboo—those three served as her storybook for all seasons; and the red peppers she hung from the rafters were there to appeal to her sons to become vigorous and virile.

By this time there were six children, born almost every two years, alternately a girl and then a boy. Together they made up games to play, at times gathering around a tree and calling out, "Money! Money! Money!" In unison they agreed and called out the same word for ten minutes or so, then jumped up and down saying, "Oh, at last! We are full of money. We are full of money!" In seconds their next words would be, "Oh, I'm tired of money."

The swings were always the spot of merriment and laughter as well as competition to see who could go the highest. The younger ones liked it best when Grandmother or Grandfather would stand behind and push them. The girls and their friends liked to jump on the low-built seesaw, bouncing one another high into the air, landing perfectly balanced on both feet to spring the other up again. Maybe this rhythmic skill somehow helped them balance heavy loads on their heads later as women.

In winter they played pick-up-the-rice-bags or rock-toss, similar to a pick-up game which Western children play with a ball and a set of jacks. Rice grains were sewn into a multicolored cloth about the size of a fist and thrown on the floor to be picked up in rhythmic numbers. Small rocks were to be picked up in ones, twos, threes, etc., between tossing another pebble into the air and catching it. No matter how often these were played, there was a challenge to improve both skill and speed. So what if it was a girl's game.

In the spring there was supposed to be a joyous celebration, but no one dreaded the Buddha's birthday on April 8 more than Yonggi, for they had to pass between the two monsters waiting at the temple gates.

That same month, on April 29, there had always been the Japanese Emperor's birthday to keep, but from this year the Koreans made that event merely a regular day on the calendar. Although Korea had to depend on the United Nations, she was not subject to Japan any more. The people destroyed the Shinto shrine in the village, not because it was the Emperor's but because it had been built by the Japanese and the villagers had been forced to buy a charm from it, put the charm in the most important room of their house and worship it morning and evening. Korea was Buddhist, not Shinto.

Anyway, on New Year's Day, 1946, the Emperor himself had announced over the radio that he was no longer a god. The eventful radio message had been formal but historically clear, in the voice of Hirohito, who would turn forty-five that year:

> We stand by the people and we wish always to share with them in their moments of joy and sorrow. The ties between us and our people have always stood upon mutual trust and affection. They do not depend upon mere legends and myths. They are not predicated on the false conception that the Emperor is divine and that the Japanese people are superior to other races, and fated to rule the world.[5]

"Myth," "false conception," "legend"—such words had a softening effect. Yonggi supposed that the Emperor's birthday could be celebrated in Japan now with greater ease, as there was not that constant dread of a god.

But he despised April 8, not because of any myth about god but because of the hideous creatures at the temple. The Buddha himself was different; the Buddha was many things to many people. But the temple was mossy and weird. Even the temple roof curved upward at each eave so as to hook the devils that might try to enter from the sky. Everything about it was frightful. Otherwise, he was glad for the lunar holiday, although he did not see why it had to be every year. As for human beings who were still alive, only three birthdays were vastly important—one on the one-hundredth day after a baby was born, another on the one-year celebration, and the other on the sixtieth year.

Nevertheless, they all put on clean socks and went to honor the Buddha.

Once inside the gate, it was all right. There was an outer court where pigeons flocked to children for peanuts. But first, just at the entrance, everybody burned a stick of incense or at least fondled the smoke that swirled abundantly upward at the brazen altar, the aroma bathing the air in its funny cedar-cinnamon sweetness. They ambled a few steps after that to the basin on the left where the water was kept running so that it was perpetually full and overflowing. Here they took a small bamboo dipper of water to their lips and rinsed their mouths, then poured the fresh water over both hands, as the hands and mouth, it was said, were the most likely defiled and in need of cleansing by the living water.

Today in the courtyard there was an extra festivity going on, where large wooden ladles were used as the visitors poured sweet tea over the statue of Buddha. At a temple more famous than this one, Yonggi heard that a special infant Buddha image was provided with tiny ladles to pour the baptismal tea over him then dip and drink from the basin he stood in. It was considered a special devotion with purifying powers, to drink the waters that had caressed his body. Strange—the Buddha was not often depicted as an infant. How many times at home Firstborn Son had repeated the words with Father, *"Kwanum Bosal!*

Namuami Tabul! Avalokitesvara, Bodhisattva"—("God-dess of mercy and god of all saints! Save us, O merciful Buddha!") Surely one's wishes could be fulfilled if the chant was kept up and the voice sounded plaintive enough.

At the nearest temple there was not the infant Buddha but another statue for touching, especially if the visitor had any infected parts or any illness which he wanted the Buddha to take away. They were to rub the part of the statue's body wherever they themselves were affected, and somehow it seemed the fortunes of health were to be granted in proportion to whatever payment or offering had transpired inside the holy place of the temple. The holy of holies was off limits. Children often amused themselves by rubbing the Buddha.

It always seemed that more children broke out with measles after Buddha's birthday. Maybe it was just that it was the measles season. Yonggi took the measles that year, too, although the disease was more common among children younger than he. At first his parents could hardly believe it was the measles, but they put him in bed because his fever went high. Unlike most cases that ran their course and then the child could get up and play, Firstborn Son stayed on the mat and had no desire to romp. Mama bathed his body with vinegar and spring water to get the fever down but he also complained of earaches. His reddened eyes were not relieved by the sunny days nor his sleeplessness by the mountain winds. It was soon to be kite-flying time in Korea, but even that could not rouse a change in the listless body that lay for weeks of little movement and zero appetite. Sometimes sleeping all day with no one able to wake him for hours, sometimes talking of hunting dragonflies in the snow, he drifted beyond a mother's communication. He did not recognize his mother or father when he looked at them.

This sickness called for another trip in the three-wheel cart. Father set out to try and persuade an old doctor of Chinese herbs to come from Pusan to have a look at his boy. Though Pusan was not over forty kilometers away, Father did not return home until all day the following sunset. The doctor would not come. From the symptoms, he had reckoned it was not worth the trip. A fragile boy like that must have developed internal inflammations, if not sleeping sickness, which would no doubt take him on before the summer ended. Even pneumonia might set in, now that he had been lying in bed for so long. The Chinese herb doctors had usually been pretty good about seeing a patient to the limits of a sickness. It was the other doctors, though there was a shortage of any kind at all, who did not want an imbalance of deaths to their credit and avoided the extremely ill. Anyway, in Korea a person was supposed to die at home and not in a hospital.

No one knew why Father had delayed so long in coming home, and no one asked. In spite of the boy's delirium, the parents smiled at times over some of his remarks. "I rode the wings of a butterfly today, and I played with a red puppy the size of my toe." His eyes looked straight ahead when he told his adventures; yet somehow he seemed to be inside those eyes, though out of touch with the family. He would fall off to sleep again, usually before Mama could get any hot soup into him. It was these sleeping spells they did not know how to cope with, as they never knew how long it would be before they could wake him and make him drink something.

A dry body that burned with fever had to have some wet food. Even when he slept, Mama dropped a little raw ginger juice with cinnamon water into his mouth. Cinnamon would help bring back an appetite, and ginger was good for old and young alike who were frail. Because he was too weak to endure any vomiting, Mama tried to make him chew on soft bran she scraped from the bamboo shoots to ward off nausea.

Long nights they watched the boy sleeping on the rice mat. He slept on, and in delirium he mumbled things they could not make out. After one story in particular, however, he took an abrupt change and announced that he was hungry. "Well, it's finally over," they understood his words to say. As if exhausted, he went on, but paused for a new breath every few words, "I knocked that dragon off the cliff. He could really wrestle. Spit out smoke in my eyes. But I finally got him. Threw him over the jagged rocks. Now, I'm hungry!" He breathed out the words, unable to lift arms or head from the mat. Mama looked at Father and dabbed at her eyes with the hem of her apron as she ran off to the kitchen to boil a slab of fish.

Mama broke the fish between her long and slender chopsticks and put a bite to Yonggi's mouth. He lay on his side, chewed the bite slowly and swallowed. She fed him rice gruel and a smile broke between her teeth as a tear fell to the floor. Her boy had come home. Their household had not suffered the curse of Firstborn Son's death. He was going to live!

3

Then Came the Communists

(1948-1954)

Ants scurried along in the crack that marred the *ondol* floor where the family used to sit. Yonggi sat staring at the energetic red ants and occasional black ones bumping along in their haste, each one dutifully carrying his load of a fly's wing. In war and peace, famine and harvest, certain creatures seemed little changed. The sun came up and the sun went down, and returned to the point of its beginning.

Like the farmhouse floor, Korea was now split by a crack that separated North from South. One war had ended and the Russians had declared a boundary, although actual fighting had not had to take place on Korean soil. Families were separated, and it seemed that the great gulf was fixed and there was to be no crossing over—except by helmeted guards, patrol dogs and ants. The border was over two hundred fifty miles away from the Cho homestead in Eonyang, and farther still from Pusan, where they now lived—all except Grandfather and Grandmother and Elder Son, who had come back to recuperate from sickness again and to hide from the Communists. Because the People's Army came down from the North and took young boys if they were big enough, families everywhere sent their sons to hide.

One of the Communists' methods of latching on to "volunteers" was to stage a youth meeting at a theater or school auditorium. There would be speeches and sometimes the showing of a Russian movie. Following the speeches, the "comrades" would call for a vote on whether or not the young men there should join the Communist army. The Communists who were planted in the meeting hall would make a good show of hands in favor of the "volunteering." Under the stern glances of the Communists, no one dared put up his hand to vote no.

After this unanimous vote the young teens would be taken right from the meeting, under the name "volunteers" and sent north somewhere to be trained as part of the People's Army. A few managed to escape en route, and when they found their way back to their town they went into complete hiding. Some were hidden in attics or under porches. Others went to relatives in the country and buried away in caves hollowed out under pigpens or other unlikely places.

In some areas they stayed in their hiding places for two or three months, until the United Nations forces recaptured the cities.

Though Yonggi was fourteen when the war broke out, his frailty and sickness were probably enough to keep him safe. If not, there was still the "lucky rice field" storage bin which Father had dug at the back of the house during the other war. A boy could fit in there if necessary.

Even Father had run from the Communists, as he was considered an "undesirable" for the Communist cause.

Somehow their knowledge penetrated even the minutest points and spanned the whole of society. When they came looking for the man who had saved the American pilot, Father dug a hole in the floor and lay in it, covering himself with Grandfather and his sleeping mat. This way, even his breathing was hidden by that of the elder man who lay above him.

In villages seized by the Communists, every house exhibited the red star of North Korea inside a white circle. As if marked by some sort of Passover blood, the lintel and two sides of the doorways bore slogans in red: "*Mansei!* A thousand years to Marshal Kim Il Sung! Our great leader! Everyone now comes under the North Korean flag!"

Some of the soldiers who walked in the cities had red stripes down their trousers. They wore strange-looking caps and carried the fat, short Russian *tabul*, the gun-of-many-bullets. The Russians had cleverly and thoroughly trained the Koreans in Siberia for five years, so that now it appeared to be only a civil war with the blond Soviets staying in the background, supplying equipment.

This was the first time a "North Korean flag" was ever heard of. The new flag was red with blue stripes along the upper and lower edges of the field, separated from the red by a fine line of white. In the center of the red flag was a large red five-pointed star on a white disc, the same red star that appeared in the flags of other Communist countries.

But Yonggi thought that flying a flag and calling a house Communist territory did not make it so. Yonggi thought the crack in the floor did not make it two floors. Nor in the beginning did the thirty-eighth parallel make the nation two Koreas.

Yet, something chaotic must have happened in Seoul. Millions of people had come from all over the peninsula seeking refuge in the southeastern tip at Pusan with their life-long possessions wrapped into a bundle on their backs or balanced on the heads of their women. Most of the nation's 20.6 million inhabitants went south to safety, including President Syngman Rhee, who had taken the newly created presidential office in 1948. The government headquarters were moved to Pusan. Korea had a saying that whoever controlled the Han River controlled Korea. The whole world seemed to be crossing the Han, though thousands were dying in their efforts. In the early evacuations some 8,000 were blown to bits by their own allies when the United Nations forces set T.N.T. to the bridge over the Han in a premature act to repress the enemy at their heels.

Seoul was taken more than once by the Communists and recaptured more than once by General Douglas MacArthur, Commander in Chief of the United Nations Command. After his surprise landing at Inchon, the U.N. took sweeping entries past the thirty-eighth parallel, taking the northern "capital," Pyongyang, and other key posts. About the time things were looking good, hordes of Chinese Communists attacked like locusts out of the Yellow Sea. By this time it was a world war in miniature, with sixteen nations sending troops to fight under the blue and white flag of the United Nations, which had just been organized at the end of World War II, in 1945. Forty nations sent medical aid and other material contributions to the Republic of Korea, while the following joined the South Korean forces: Australia, Belgium, Great Britain, Canada, Colombia, Ethiopia, France, Greece, Luxembourg, the Netherlands, New Zealand, the Philippines, Thailand, Turkey, South Africa, and the United States.

But if the Chinese lacked anything in modern equipment, they made up for it in tactics and numbers. Though wave after wave of frontline Chinese fell before the steel of those they invaded, there were droves of others just like them who kept coming. Even in unlikely places where a battle was not in progress, a farmer's cart might be seen passing a U.N. camp, as an innocent-looking coolie would be on his way to the pumpkin patch. If he was close enough, he used the grenade he wore hidden under his shirt, usually a suicidal mission in which he gloriously took several Americans with him.

Four times in five centuries invaders had attacked the Korean capital. But the last time, Seoul was 80 percent destroyed by gunfire, bombing, and incendiary blazes set by the Communists during the Korean War. During the Chinese Communist occupation of Seoul, the city that had a prewar population of a million and a half dwindled to 150,000. Approximately 35,000 houses were completely destroyed and another 20,000 damaged. Fifteen thousand commercial and business-industrial buildings were razed and another 8,000 partly destroyed. Churches, schools, and other public buildings likewise suffered from the general destruction. Seoul was dying.

Father had been wise to live in the southern mountains during the Japanese peak. Because he hated taking their orders, he had moved away from Pusan to become a tiller of the soil in a village unknown to the world.

"But I hate this place!" Yonggi crushed an ant with his finger and got up to go outside as he muttered it again. "You hear me? I hate you, peaches!" By now a restless adolescent, he poked a finger through the white paper door and sauntered outside.

Taking his perch in the open-air hut to guard the orchard, the gangling, scrawny teen-ager settled down to read a book he had brought back from Pusan. It was *War and Peace*, by Leo Tolstoy. How appropriate he had thought the title was, with a Russian author, in an English translation, and all of Korea cancerous with the raging "civil war." He set out to read it in spite of the language. Determined to know the language of the Americans who had liberated them from Japan, he "read" page by page, some pages a hundred times, so that eventually he could memorize phrases of English, tidbits of meaning seeming to float up before him.

"The next time I fight you, black boy, I'll at least know how to talk your words," he said aloud in his own Korean. It was not pleasant to remember that night when the black American sailor had beaten him to a pulp in Pusan. It was at the docks, where Yonggi had loaded freight on the night shift to pay his junior high schooling and high school tuition. He did not quite remember what had started the fight, but that night he had felt he was going to die of pain. The most vivid recollection was of not being able to catch his next breath. Even worse than the blood and bruises, was his inability to breathe and an awful clutching at nothingness in a desperate reach for air.

He started to read again as he lay on the rice-straw mats

in the gazebo-shaped grass hut among the peach trees. But as he looked down at the book, a long snake was stretching toward his face from the mat under his belly. In gasping terror, he could only stare in fright at the creature for what seemed like unending moments of threatening horror. When the snake finally gave up and slithered away, Yonggi lay in a cold sweat, trembling throughout his body.

Grandmother had seen it and dashed toward the gazebo, pointing wildly but unable to scream.

It was not the first time a snake had scared him so. As a child he had stepped on one in the bamboo patch out back. But that time his bare feet had jumped off and run as soon as they felt the stranger wiggle.

It was war and peace, all right; and at this point Yonggi felt life was more at war than at peace. It was one struggle after another, and even now he was not healthy. While other boys played and wrestled, Yonggi sat thinking. He longed for a friend, but no one liked to talk of ideas about life and death nor read what someone else had thought. Loneliness drove him to books, or perhaps books drove him to loneliness. But books were not easy for a boy with no money to get. Struggle, struggle, struggle.

Since President Rhee's "land reforms" the Chos had lost most of their holdings and the new liberation government was not strong enough to make good their promises between the Japanese colonial evacuation and the Communist War. Father was more bitter than before because of Grandfather's stubborn denial of a formal education.

Maybe Confucius was right. Maybe there was hope in the ancient philosopher's idea that all being, everything, resulted from the combination of the negative influence and the positive influence, *Um* and *Yang*.[6] These two opposing forces unite to form one perfect cell which then divides to produce new cells that continue to reproduce in geometric progression. For 2,500 years the teachings of Confucius had affected perhaps more human beings than those of any other thinker. Tomes of his sayings had been memorized by Chinese students for more than twenty centuries. Though Korea held to her own identity and was vastly different from China, the umbilical knot was hard to cast away. Even the very name "Cho" was almost pure Chinese and was later sometimes mistakenly connected with Chou En-lai. Confucius was nevertheless the mainstay of Korean thought.

But to say that everything resulted from the combination of the negative agent and the positive agent, was a flagrant assumption. Somewhere there had to be a positive force, and so far life seemed an imbalance on the negative side. Where was justice?

He remembered one day when he had been down at the U.S. Navy coal cars on the railroad line in Pusan. He hated going there because it was such a dirty place. But mostly he hated the poverty that forced him to make this errand in order for Mama to have fuel for cooking. He hated for the other boys to meet him coming back carrying his bucket of coal. He hated their rubbing it on him and teasing him about being a poor black beggar. Deeper than all of that, it was the need to steal that he abhorred.

"Well, Confucius, what about this one? Do you have an answer? One day a man came with his seven-year-old boy. The man's wife had been killed in the war. The boy was scratching out the coal and his father was collecting it when the M.P.s came. So the boy jumped down. One big chunk went between the tracks, a really good chunk. The boy went in after it. The train began to move. People shrieked, but no one tried to save that boy. Suddenly one man ran in and threw the boy out. It was his father. As the boy was saved, the man was trapped and the train kept moving. He had dived into that place between the tracks to save his boy. I heard his backbone break. Then his belly burst open. I saw it. What about that orphan now, Confucius—is he a negative or a positive?

"I'll tell you what he is—he is a hungry Korean boy who is going to grow up skillful in one thing, the art of stealing. You can't eat positives and negatives." In philosophy where was there reality? In reality where was there beauty? In beauty where was there permanence?

In the transients, there were certainly enough constants. As sure as the square root of 144 is twelve, there was war, and TB, orphans, and snakes, and hungry stomachs—and peach fuzz and worms, and woodpeckers. The whole purpose for living seemed to be for the sole aim of dying. "I refuse that idea! I reject it!" he said aloud to himself. "And I reject a life of disease and poverty. I rise above the condition of myself! Poverty might be somebody's square root, but it is sure not going to be mine!" Yonggi got louder. "Someday I'm not going to be ragged and poor! I'm going to be a medical doctor."

In the absence of health, he turned his life ambitions to medicine. If this had anything to do with the negative-positive combination, Confucius had been over-credited as the originator of the balance of powers. Surely somewhere there must be some force that could help him to achieve.

"I've been a nobody long enough; now I am going to be a medical doctor," he repeated as if saying it again would make it so. As he said it, a spider fell almost to the mat, going up and down on a single thread like a yo-yo. Yonggi watched as it climbed up and fell again. How like Korea, he thought. Survive one war to fall into another and hang by a thread from her innermost being to try to pull back up. The Communists were as ruthless as the Japanese had been, even though the same Korean blood ran in their veins.

In fact, in some parts the people were saying that the Japanese occupation had been better. At least, the Japanese had built bridges, not bombed them. They had built railroads, highways, telegraph lines, telephones, power dams, six-story buildings, streetcar systems, ports and docks. They established agriculture experimental stations in the South and industry in the North; they improved public health and sanitation.

"The Japanese never bothered me," reminisced an old man in Pusan. "They gave me a new name and made me speak Japanese but they caused me no harm. They did take away my rice, but we could manage to hide away whatever we had to have. The Japanese made me work without pay during the war, building the airfield, but we ate from their barrels. They put my son in the Imperial Army, but they gave him warm shirts and good shoes."

Indeed among the older Koreans there were some who did not seem to care one way or the other whether their country was Communist or democratic, whatever was meant by either. They wanted shelter, food and family, and the dream of every man was to have a plot of land, though many would pull their own plows. It was not uncommon for the aged to keep two flags, one representing the North Korean People's "democracy," and the other the Republic of Korea. One was kept hidden, depending on which side was in control of the village.

Motivated by survival and driven by hardships, a people could learn the art of answering questions with answers the examiners wanted to hear.

All the way to what became known as the Pusan perimeter, troops had come down from the North, ultimately from Russia, where they had trained. Yonggi hated them; and he hated his father for not being able to send him to high school, because of them. He hated his father for giving Mama too many children, too, because that had meant Elder Son must give up school or combine it with odd jobs of all sorts, wearing himself out at night work on the dirty docks. Father ran for office in the general assembly, spending all his money for that campaign, and failed. Yonggi hated him for failing.

Eonyang being only forty kilometers from Pusan and her war-infested harbors, the comings and goings of war were a constant threat even to the mountain folk. Soldiers from both sides tramped through the orchards stripping the peach trees just as the fruit was fully ripe. Hardly one peach could be seen on the trees after the soldiers were finished. Only the fragrance remained, mixed with those left rotting on the ground. In a way Cho thought he should have been relieved; instead he was at once sad and at the same time angry.

"All is futile," he said.

The Korean War had been going on since that Sunday

dawn, June 25, 1950. "It's useless to try to wait it out here. The peaches are gone. All the days of my youth will be gone too, while I sit and shoo away the birds for the next soldiers."

He shook the can of stones he held in his hand. Meant to rattle and scare the birds, it was a simple device but he held it high and rattled it today as if ringing a bell to toll the death of Yonggi Cho, the nobody. He was through tending peaches.

"I'll go back to Pusan. I'll go to school, war or no war. I'll find a way!"

Cho was seventeen when a delegation at Panmunjom, heretofore an unheard of village midway between North and South, declared a halt to the war on July 27, 1953. In thirty-seven months, 58,000 South Korean soldiers had been killed and 176,000 had been wounded. More than a million civilians had been killed, and another million had been wounded or injured. The war left 100,000 Korean orphans and more than 284,000 widows, with 517,000 dependent children. About eight million South Koreans were driven from their homes, and 595,000 homes were demolished.[7]

More than two million refugees streamed across the mountains to the South side, most of them risking their lives if seen by the Russian patrol guards. A two-and-a-half-mile demilitarized zone had been designated, stretching 155 miles roughly east and west, and in this vacuum hardly a lizard dared move. Little did Cho suspect that his future wife was among the multitudes who crossed over in the night, family-by-family, inch-by-inch.

In fact, many forces of his future were being shaped in the crises of the fifties, though he had had his own private wars to fight. In Pusan he went back to high school and tutored English on the side, learning as he did so. Working and studying, working and studying. Would there never be more time to study? Because his body tired out so, he had had to find other work besides the dock.

Yet all of Korea was out finding work. The war had ended and millions migrated south to Pusan. Millions more were returning from their temporary asylum in Pusan to start all over in Seoul. President Rhee, who had gained disfavor by prematurely releasing over 25,000 prisoners of war to the Communists, had been among the first to return to the capital. For five years the South had had their own President and constitution, and the North theirs.

Like a potato that goes into decay to give food for the buds, Choson disappeared and in 1948 the Republic of Korea (South) and the Democratic People's Republic of Korea (North) had sprung into being. The war seemed merely to seal the arrangement as if dipping one's *tojang* (signature stamp) to sign it in blood.

Yet the land had not changed. The mountains were as rugged as before. The people themselves were settling and resettling. Since the Liberation from Japan, almost four million northern refugees altogether were looking for a place in the South. In one decade these migrations reduced the population of North Korea from nearly thirteen million in 1944 to 8.3 million as of 1954. In 1954, the population of South Korea challenged the already deficient food supply with 21.8 million inhabitants.

According to estimates of the South Korean government, 1.4 million emigrants returned from Japan and 430,000 from other areas, mainly China, as of January,

1950.

After the Korean War, the new nation was also faced with a new breed: social welfare institutions alone reported taking care of 24,000 mixed-blood children in one given year.

South Korea was teeming with people. Would she become a toy of any despot strong enough to take her and hold her? Or would the people lock arms and stand, to make her their own? As one whole, Korea had not been large, but now South Korea became a runt country, lying in the sea. Yet within her boundaries were the remnants of her forefathers and the seeds of her grandchildren.

The sole thing which Koreans wanted was oneness. Now that seemed destined to never be so. One nation, one people. How could they exist as two? The North, which had been developed for industry, needed food from the warmer climate of the South. The South depended on the North for electricity and coal. Parents in the North had helped their children escape to the South: "Try to find Uncle so-and-so."

Signs were scribbled on toilet walls or stuck in the ground near river crossings: "Looking for the family of so-and-so." "Anybody kin to me, meet me in Taegu."

Like an earthworm that has been cut in half, both sides of Korea would wiggle into the dirt and accept the life that remained—peace without unification.

Gunfire was no longer spitting out from every direction, and Koreans had learned to be thankful for that. They lived and had their children always in the shadow of the threat of war. Perhaps it was as much as any nation on the fringe of two Communist countries could expect.

New cemeteries marred the serene beauty of the land;

and scarecrows did not wear the worn-out straw hats of last year, but the steel helmets of dead soldiers. Korea had poured out her lifeblood, and her friends had given selflessly. Over and above the hundreds of thousands of South Koreans who died, 32,693 foreign soldiers died fighting for freedom on Korean soil in the three-year struggle, and 119,336 foreign soldiers were listed as wounded or missing.

Fighting for the other side, an estimated 900,000 Chinese soldiers were killed, wounded or missing, along with 520,000 North Koreans.[8]

But the living must go on. With babies and bundles strapped to their backs, a million-and-a-half people moved over the country. For many, the direction did not matter; for most, they aimed for the other side of the Han River. They had miles to go and weeks of trudging over rocks and barren hills. Some tied rags around their feet to protect their rubber slippers from too many cuts and gashes on the jagged stones. This time they were not driven by tanks or bombs exploding behind them, but by something inside each one of them. It was not the hardships they had to fear—these were proof that the spirit had not died. It was when they stopped moving that they had to fear. If a man stopped too long, that was the time to fear. Every man had to stumble forward and ache to keep stumbling forward. It was a good sign. Confucius had said that a commander may be snatched away from his army, but the will cannot be taken from the humblest man.

Hence, they were everywhere. If not making a way back to a plot of land somewhere, where hundreds of years of family records were buried in pots beneath the ground, then they were trying to find work to do in the city or at the docks. A man has to work; he has to do something with his hands and with his mind.

By now English was coming more easily to Cho Yonggi, and he got another tutoring job on the side. But his own health had not picked up and he had been forced to delay his studies. Was he destined to become a high-school drop-out?

His coughing got worse and he could tell he was weaker than before. While doing chin-ups at school he had fainted and blood had filled his mouth. For a long time he had been used to one meal a day, but his condition was more serious than something caused by poor eating habits. The fruit he carried around to sell on the streets felt heavier and his breath became shorter. As a common fruit vendor, he was able to observe all kinds of humanity. Hunger and the struggle to survive tended to make everyone equal at some point. But he regretted it was his lot to associate mostly with the fruit vendors and others equally poor, for he thought a man tended to become like those whom he saw and lived around. Yet illness was no respecter of persons. Seeing an old man scuttle along for a few feet, then stop to rest on his cane, Yonggi suddenly realized that at eighteen he was doing almost the same thing.

One afternoon he fell, fruit and all, and vomited blood. Blood had filled his mouth before; it had happened one day while he was teaching English. But this time the salty taste kept filling his mouth as more blood came up from his chest. Scared to keep lying there and scared to get up, he pressed his hands quickly against his mouth, but then the blood gushed from his nose. Strangling like a choked animal, he lapsed into unconsciousness.

Not knowing how long he had lain helpless, he awoke with his clothes soaked in blood. Almost too weak to stand, he managed to crawl home. He looked around and the sky appeared black. His own hand was as white as paper and he knew he had lost a lot of blood.

All night long he was in and out of a coma. His fever ran rampant and when he coughed, he choked on the blood that issued forth. By morning he felt more dead than alive.

Father and Mama prayed to the Buddha. No answer came. In the troubled lives of his grandparents as well as his own family, he could not say he had ever seen them receive any answers to their supplications.

They took him to the hospital, already overcrowded with disease-ridden patients. After x-rays and what seemed endless waiting, the doctor called the Cho family back into the office and looked deeply at Yonggi. "Young man, I have to be honest with you," said the man in white, representing the very profession Cho Yonggi aspired to enter. "Is there anything you would particularly like to eat?"

"Doctor, what a question! The war is barely over. Three meals a day are impossible. How can I expect to eat some special food?" Yonggi answered.

The doctor did not look at his patient but asked a second question. "Then is there any relative you would especially like to meet?"

"No, doctor."

"I am very sorry to say this, but we can do nothing for you. At the most, you have three more months to live, if that long." The doctor hung his head.

Yonggi wanted to speak. He wanted to scream out at all

the medicines that lined the shelves. He looked at his own ribs and wondered why a hospital full of medicine could not help an eighteen-year-old to live. What was happening?

"You can see the picture for yourself. Your right lung looks like a honeycomb; your left lung has wasted away. There is no way possible to save what's left of it."

Yonggi could only stare at the doctor.

"No use to put this one in the hospital," the doctor shrugged and gestured toward the x-rays, as if reading the youth's questions. "It's just a waste of medicine to use it on a consumption case like this." Speaking in the third person made it easier. "And anyway there's no medicine to help."

Acute pulmonary tuberculosis. TB. Consumption.

Yonggi went back home dazed. Unbearably fatigued, he could only lie in bed and cough. Mornings were the best, and his fever usually waited until afternoon to burn him with its heat.

Yonggi used the mornings to make a calendar, a three-month calendar, and he hung it up and waited.

At night the coughing became incessant. It would stop only with the rush of blood and that familiar salty sputum. His arms looked skinny even to himself, and at times it was easier to lie limp than to try and squeeze out a cool cloth for his head.

He counted his pulse. He counted specks on the ceiling and anything there was to count on the walls. At times he wanted to live. At other times he wished it did not take so long to die.

He thought about the Buddha. He thought about the

doctor. He thought about medicine. And with every thought, he wanted to cry out in protest. He was afraid and desperate. His eyes wide with fear, one night he cried out to the ceiling, "Is there any God?"

He listened.

"If there is anyone called God in the universe, please come! I do not ask you to save my physical life—that would be too much to expect—but I want you to come and make me ready to die!"

On a day when he was coughing up blood and feverish, Yonggi was startled to see a girl come into his room and sit down. When he had heard her knock on the door, he would never have guessed he had a female visitor. In Korea the women were held in low esteem, the men being always superior. She carried a Bible in her hand, but she was only an eighteen-year-old girl. Bitterly, Yonggi ordered her to leave. The audacity of such a woman! Coming so boldly into the very presence of a man!

"Get out!" he said as he pointed weakly to the door.

"Sir, I have a heavy heart for this house. I could not help but come. Something in me compelled me to come here. I had no idea why I was so drawn to this house when I was passing by. Now I see, you are a dying man. So I want to tell you about Jesus Christ, my Savior."

"Oh, you Christian dog! You dirty Christian! Get out of my house!" he yelled.

She spoke firmly. "Until you accept Jesus Christ, I will never leave. You have no strength at all; I am stronger than you. Even if you push me, I will not go out of your house."

In spite of her strength, she radiated a smile, and even

Yonggi in his arrogance could see the peace on her face. But as she began to talk about Jesus, he became more and more angry. Infuriated, he cursed her in both English and Korean. He threatened her by saying that the millions of TB germs which were coming from his mouth would infect her and she would also die by being slowly consumed away, the same as he.

Immovable, she replied, "My Jesus will protect me."

She read from the Bible, despite his unwillingness to hear. She prayed. And she sang a song. She kept up this routine until evening, with a continuous background of coughing and moaning. At dark she left.

As the door closed behind her, Yonggi uttered, "Bless Buddha, she has gone."

4

Dying to Live
(1954)

He spent the night alone. Waiting. Listening. Too tired to sleep, too exhausted not to. Would he die tomorrow? How would he know when the moment came?

Father had reminded him of the central message of Buddhism, that there is no reality except in nothingness. To attain that blissful state of nirvana was the goal of every man, if he was a true follower of Gautama Buddha. Yonggi had been taught the Buddhist chants and sutras from early childhood, the rhythmic monotones designed to lull one into that state of oblivion, the extinction of the self.

"Nothing is real," Father had said to him. "There is no life and no death, no joy and no sorrow—only in Buddha is there reality. Forget about life and death and have peace."

If nothing is real, then what about this awful headache? He pounded his head and tried to turn onto his other side. What about the pain in his leg muscles and in his chest? The coughing was real, the mouthfuls of blood were real, the smell of his room was real.

The doctor had said that the tuberculosis had attacked like a blitzkrieg throughout his body. By now he knew it was true.

He set his mind to memorizing Chinese characters. By setting an unrealistic goal he might at least avoid thinking. He would not stop with less than a hundred characters a day, though it made his father angry to catch him studying instead of resting. Father was a man of many books. Why should he be upset? Father had read *Tao Te Ching* and other classics of Chinese philosophy and had pretty well taught them to Eldest Son through the years. Yonggi would not be deterred from this one activity he had set for himself, to memorize three thousand Chinese characters before he died. The most direct act he thought he ever saw his father do was the night Father caught Yonggi hiding his studies under the blanket. "Oh, go ahead and study if you must! Don't hide your studies from me under the blanket; the candle may catch the blanket on fire."

Another morning came. And so did the girl. Anger boiled up inside him, but he had little fight left in him. She seated herself and began to pray. She sang several songs quietly and read the Bible as if to an audience. Yonggi cursed, and she said nothing as a comeback. Like the previous day, it was evening before she left.

The next morning she came again.

"Girl, when are you going to leave me alone?" he mumbled out the words without looking at her.

"Not until you accept the message of Jesus Christ, because I cannot stand this heaviness in my heart."

Yonggi turned to look at her. What was this? A Bible had been placed beside his bed. A Bible! That awful book which the Japanese soldiers had burned as being revolutionary. It claimed that some King was coming to set up a kingdom that would even supersede the Japanese Empire of that time. The Bible. That awful book, representing religion, which Karl Marx had labeled "an opium of the people." With every ounce of waning energy left in him, Yonggi picked up the book and flung it at her feet, ordering her to take her cheap religion and get out of his room.

She left. But every day she came back. On the fifth day, when the slight knock on the door came, and the girl entered as usual, Yonggi noticed something different beginning to happen. He was almost glad to see her. She was different from anyone he had ever met. She was persistent, but not troubled. He observed her for a long time. Whether she looked straight ahead or at her Bible, whether she prayed or sat perfectly silent, she somehow kept a serene but joyful countenance. There seemed to be a ray of happiness in her eyes.

"Well," he spoke at last, "I want to ask you one question. Why do you come to me? I am dying, as you can see if you have eyes." (He now weighed about half his normal weight.) "It is stupid to pray for me. Why do you pray?"

She answered softly, "Humanly speaking, I could never like you nor come near you, but I have someone who lives in me and He constrains me to come here and pray for you."

Someone who lives in you? Now he knew she was crazy. "Who is he?" he asked, half smiling.

"My Jesus." She began to cry.

In the presence of the tears rolling silently down her face, Yonggi could not be his obstinate self. He, too, began to cry. Completely forgetting who he was, he cried, and he kept on crying.

At last he said to her, "Your Jesus—whoever He is—I want to know Him."

Looking up through her tears she handed her Bible to the figure on the mat and he took it.

"Here is the whole answer for you," she said as she pressed it into his hands.

As he opened it to page one, she snatched it from him and quickly flipped the pages to a section well past the middle of the book. "Please," she said, "you do not have time to start in Genesis. Before you reach Revelation, you will be a dead man. This is urgent. You have to read the Gospels first."

Turning to the book of Matthew, she gave him the Bible again. Beginning to read, he curled his lips as a sign of distaste. "This is like a telephone directory. How can I read this?" he grumbled.

She explained that all of the names listed in chapter one were her ancestors and that each one held a special place in her heart, but for now she recommended that Cho skip those names and go on reading, assuring him that he would find a tremendous story.

After a few pages he looked up and complained it was hard to comprehend. Even if he read it more than once, there were places that did not make sense to him. He would rather study Chinese.

"Sir," she spoke in a kind voice but as one having

authority, "do you like to eat fish?"

What kind of question was that? "Sure, you lunatic girl, of course I like to eat fish."

"When you are eating fish, do you eat the bones?"

"Of course not; I pick the bones with my chopsticks and eat the white flesh."

"Then please read this Bible the same way," she coaxed. "When you find bones, pick around those bones and find the meat you can eat."

With that, the girl said a blessing and went away. He never saw her again, nor knew her name. She had left a book in his hands. He expected it to be full of tedious prayers and rituals and to dwell on the details of an involved philosophy in the manner of Buddhist literature. He was not eager to take on the task of such heavy reading.

Yet this book seemed to possess a glow. It was a book which seemed to possess a magnetic force that drew him to it.

Once when it fell from his hands, he picked it up and started to read where it had fallen open: "Though I walk through the valley of the shadow of death, I will fear no evil: for thou art with me; thy rod and thy staff they comfort me. Thou preparest a table before me" (Ps. 23:4, 5).

He slept. Unable to find that page again, he turned back to Matthew, the place where the girl had told him to read. Surprised to find that the Bible centered on that man whom she had called "my Jesus," he was further surprised that this book called Jesus the Son of God. In Korean there is one word for "God" which means "the one God" *(Hananim)* as opposed to the Japanese word

Kamisama, referring to any of eight million gods. But this was the first he had heard of the son of *Hananim.* It was easy to understand. Yonggi was the son of Cho. Jesus was the son of *Hananim.* Jesus was not a philosophy, after all. He was not a ritual nor a doctrine. He was flesh and blood.

The book never talked about Christianity, nor religion.

Yonggi Cho forgot about his coughing and his weakness. It was as if he began eating again, this time from the Bible itself. He felt thirsty but not parched.

The Bible made a lot of sense. It talked about Jesus as one who gave living water, or life-giving water, to anyone and everyone who would ask Him. In Chinese philosophy which Koreans memorized, Tao Te Ching had said, "In the world there is nothing more submissive and weak than water. Yet for attacking that which is hard and strong nothing can surpass it. This is because there is nothing that can take its place. That the weak overcomes the strong, And the submissive overcomes the hard, Everyone in the world knows yet no one can put this knowledge into practice."[9]

Here was a man, this Jesus, who just might be the one to put all this into practice. Anyway, Jesus had a truth about Him which Yonggi liked to think about. Life-giving water, submissively taking on the shape of whatever container would hold it and give it form. In this water was there life itself? Could a human body become that container and the life-water take on that human shape?

This Jesus went into people's homes, too. He went into some homes to eat with them, into other homes to help the sick and dying. And no one died when He was around. Throughout childhood, Yonggi had questioned and never found the answer to his probing, "What is life? Where is life?" Could it be that in the radius of this man's presence, therein was the source of life? Had *Hananim* sent life in the universe by way of Jesus? Strange. But the one thing Jesus went about giving out was life, aliveness. Everywhere.

It was like a fantasy. Yet there was enough suffering and crowding in that world at Galilee and Jerusalem to make it more than fantasy. Somehow fantasy and reality were able to touch.

"If only I could come to that man Jesus," Yonggi said aloud. "Why, even this cough would disappear and my body would rest. My blood would stop pouring out and I could catch a deep breath and live."

But he grew despondent. As quickly as the surge of hope had risen in him, despair set in. His mind started reasoning away the odds. He could never come to Jesus. Jesus had lived two thousand years ago. But even if the man was still in Jerusalem, Yonggi remembered cursing that Christian girl and throwing the Bible across the room onto the floor. He had hated Christianity. Now because he was dying would he shamefully hold out his hand and expect Jesus to help him? If it were not for his consumption, he suspected he would never have considered Christianity for a moment.

Suddenly it was not a matter of Buddha or Christ, tradition or treason. It was a matter of life or death. The calendar hung on a nail before his bed—one month and it would all be over.

In desperation he turned again to the Bible, this time searching for something to prove Jesus hated him because He hated sinners. That was a new word—"sinners"—but reading had told him what it meant. He looked and looked. Nowhere could he find in one instance that Jesus hated sinful people. Instead, He forgave an adulteress and set her free. He had not even hated the Roman soldiers who nailed Him to a cross and rolled dice for the coat off His back. Everywhere He gave people a second chance and then confirmed it with *Hananim,* His Father.

He was like some go-between to represent the people on earth before *Hananim.* In the Orient a go-between arranged marriages, as love was usually a result of marriage instead of marriage being a result of love. A go-between is also used in Asian business transactions and especially regarding decisions or problems involving two companies. Yonggi had thought Christianity was a foreign religion, but the Bible showed that Jesus was from the East.

In Korea an interpreter was needed since the war, whenever an American military or political leader held discussions with Koreans. The middleman sometimes spoke for both parties, interchanging from one language to the other. Jesus seemed to be likewise interpreting what *Hananim* wanted to say to man, and also what things man wanted to say to *Hananim.* What a fascinating arrangement!

"Jesus, you even healed lepers. Can you heal my TB?" Yonggi had said it before he realized it. The sound of his own voice seemed to vibrate throughout his body. It reminded him of a night a few weeks earlier when he had cried out for anyone in the universe who might be God. Was it possible that God had really heard? Was it possible that God himself had sent that girl to his room that smelled of blood and reeked of sweat? No, of course not. A majestic God of the universe would never condescend to use a lowly woman for His messenger. No, that would never happen.

A stupid thought.

Yet, it *was* a woman—even the adulteress herself—whom Jesus had sent back to tell the men about himself. Where was that story? John, chapter four, in the New Testament.

As suddenly as he had spoken, that ever-tickling raspiness in his throat cleared away and a soothing, vibrant stirring started in his chest. If this was death, it was a wonderful feeling. Somehow it felt like a warm hand gently massaging his chest with a lotion; while his whole being relaxed, his thirsty body drank of the soothing lotion, first the chest, the back and shoulders, down the arms and over each hand, then his aching legs. In the soft mystery of this soothing wonder, he fell asleep as a baby on a trip, wanting to see what was going on but unable to keep his eyelids open. It was a restful sleep, the kind which feels good upon awaking.

He looked the same. His room was the same. But for the first time in over seventy days he felt an urge to get up and walk. When he raised his head from the pillow there was no pounding headache to keep him down. He stood up and slowly walked about the room. He wanted to sing! But no words would come out. In all of his teachings, he knew only the Buddhist chants but they were all a pessimistic, dark sound, completely inadequate to express anything that bubbled within him now.

His parents had stayed away as much as possible and kept the other children away from the contaminated room. Now they wondered at this strange delirium and knew the end was surely not far away. They coaxed him back to bed and reminded him that he looked like a skeleton.

Day after day he felt stronger. When he could gain enough energy to go back to the doctor for another examination, he determined that was what he would do. It took time. He walked a little each day. Children ran from him at first and called him a white corpse or a ghost. He straightened up and breathed in the fresh air. He wondered where the girl had gone, the one who had prayed and read the Bible to him. He wished he had paid attention when she prayed. Surely there was someone in all of Korea who could tell him how to communicate with God. He knew he could not call directly on *Hananim* any more than he could call directly on President Rhee or General MacArthur. There must be some protocol, some procedure. The Bible told of Jesus instructing His disciples to go into all the world, even to the uttermost parts of the earth. Certainly there was someone in Korea.

Christ had come into the world to make a way for sinners, not to call the perfect. Yonggi had told a lot of lies—not big ones, but little ones that served to make him appear better in some way than he actually was. In fact, he did not know any person who had not stolen something or cheated on a test at least once. They were not terribly bad, he thought; nevertheless, having done so made them less than perfect and therefore in need of Jesus to represent them before *Hananim.*

He guessed that was the one thing that made him equal to that girl. Even a Korean man stood helplessly in need of *Hananim's* son, because the Bible said that God looks on the inside of man's heart instead of on the outward appearance. Anyway, by now Yonggi could find something again in that Book if he had read it before. A sentence in that letter to the Galatians had startled him: "For as many of you as have been baptized into Christ have put on Christ. There is neither Jew nor Greek, there is neither bond nor free, there is neither male nor female: for ye are all one in Christ Jesus" (Gal. 3:27-28).

He no longer felt contempt for the girl. Instead, he felt admiration for her because she had transcended the binds of tradition to obey a higher law. What courage it must have taken!

What courage it must have taken for Jesus, too, to live a supernatural life in the natural environment of other men, and finally to end it in the humiliating death on the cross as a Roman criminal. What kind of Father was it who could give up His own son as the substitute for others?

"Ye believe in God, believe also in me," Jesus had said. "In my Father's house are many mansions: if it were not so, I would have told you. I go to prepare a place for you. And if I go and prepare a place for you, I will come again, and receive you unto myself; that where I am, there ye may be also. And whither I go ye know, and the way ye know. I am the way, the truth, and the life: no man cometh unto the Father, but by me" (John 14:1-4, 6).

In Korean the Bible said, "I am the road." A road was never made to be looked at but to be traveled. One must try it to find out where it really goes, for at no point can the traveler see the end; unless he has walked that road and come to know it, can he fully trust it. Yonggi knew that if a man born in the Middle East had called himself "the road," then that man was meaning for people to follow the road, not to sit and look at it, nor merely to study it and analyze it. Yonggi had a move to make; you don't follow roads by lying in bed thinking about them.

How simple. "A terrace nine storeys high Rises from hodfuls of earth; A journey of a thousand miles Starts from beneath one's feet," was memorized by all Tao scholars.[10] How similar to Eastern thought the Bible seemed. To get to some point out there where this Jesus was trying to get us to go, you have to start with step one. Jesus talked a lot about personal victories, success and health. Was He trying to take us to that point?

"Savour that which has no flavor. Do good to him who has done you an injury," read the ancient Chinese codes. "Ye are the salt of the earth," said Jesus (Matt. 5:13).

"Love your enemies," He said again, "bless them that curse you, do good to them that hate you, and pray for them which despitefully use you, and persecute you; That ye may be the children of your Father which is in heaven: for he maketh his sun to rise on the evil and on the good, and sendeth rain on the just and on the unjust. For if ye love them which love you, what reward have ye? do not even the publicans the same?" (Matt. 5:44-46)

Likewise, Taoist thought went: "Those who are good I treat as good. Those who are not good I also treat as good. In so doing I gain in goodness."[11]

Tao and his contemporary, Confucius, disagreed on certain key points, and this thing about loving one's enemies was one of them. Someone asked, "What do you think about the principle that injury should be repaid with kindness?"

"With what then will you repay kindness?" quipped the Confucian master. "Repay injury with justice and kindness with kindness." The doctrine of universal love would mean there was no special affection, then, due one's father.[12]

In places so different, in other places so alike—the Bible and Eastern philosophies.

At Golgotha, Jesus died on a cross, crucified by soldiers of the Roman Empire. Encyclopedias claimed that in three days He rose again. Herod could not kill Him, and the grave could not hold Him. Like a plant that falls into the ground to die at the right time, Jesus died so that new life could come up in all who dared identify with Him. Eastern philosophy contained some worthwhile ideals; but Jesus enabled man to actually do them.

In one point of grave difference, the Easterner who is generally group-oriented tends to avoid facing personal, individual responsibility for sin, whereas the Bible calls every person to account before God. In the East, Cho thought, the clubs, the families, the peers absorb personal errors. Hence one's code or standard lies with the ideas of those about him; however, the Bible presents God as the standard, regardless of what others may say. It would never be a wishy-washy standard, changing as groups change. Truth was truth.

There were times when the corners of the one-page calendar hung like hands being crucified from the nail at the foot of Yonggi Cho's bedroll. One month had been left on the calendar but even that month had gone by and the corpse still had life. He had left the calendar blowing in the wind, as every breath gave promise of life and the continuity of life. Jesus himself had given life as His reason for coming to earth: "I am come that they might have life, and that they might have it more abundantly" (John 10:10).

"Mister Jesus, thank you," was all Cho could say.

At last Yonggi was able to make his way to the doctor's office, where the prognosis had been pronounced: death in three months. The doctor slowly drew his own head back and sat looking strangely at his patient. After extensive x-rays he had no explanation except a shrug of his hands and shoulders, "I don't know where it went or what happened, but there is no evidence that your body has ever had TB. Strangest thing! Not only that, but your heart seems to be normal size, whereas before, it was abnormally enlarged. This is a medical wonder! You are a new man!"

Yonggi could hardly wait to tell Father and Mama. It was really true—he was going to live. Smiling as he entered where the family sat, he spoke as if back from a distant country. Life had been going on as usual with its cares of the day, and they had not experienced the same adventures he wanted desperately to share with them now. They had drifted apart, and the thing that made them apart was not physical but mental. The things he told them that evening glowed upon his face like the brightness of the kerosene lamp illuminating the tiny room. Mama shook her head from side to side and softly uttered a prophetic word as if drawing a curtain between them, "That boy will become famous by the time he is twenty-three."

Father sat in silence, merely tapping with his hand on the edge of the table.

In Korea, those who follow Jesus Christ cease all prayers to the spirits of their ancestors and stop going to the temple to make intercession for the dead.

Yet it was for this cause that Cho Yonggi had been born. As Firstborn Son, it was his filial duty to take proper care of Father and Mama after their death, as well as to provide sons to perpetuate the proper rites from generation to generation. Of all their nine children, it was the disgrace of all times for this one, Firstborn Son, to engage in heresy. He could not be true to Korea if he broke sacred traditions. Better to have a dead son than filial impiety. After all that Grandfather had done for him, how could he renounce his own duties?

To break from tradition was like accusing the ancestors of being wrong. One was expected to stand with one's father even if his father lied; if a father said a matter was white, the son would say so, too, even if in truth it were gray or yellow or even black. So what if Jesus was the truth and the way? Facts nor truth, God nor man must never cause a breach in the family.

The wick burned high and the tall glass chimney smoked up. Those kerosene lamps gave out a bright, white light, but if things were not adjusted just right they smoked up and turned the crystal thin chimney black with soot.

Next day Big Sister was first to his side. "Brother, do you love that Jesus more than you love our family? Would you give us up for Him?"

Yonggi knew that the hand of Father had pounced. Koreans lived in dreadful fear of five great elements: thunder, floods, lightning, fires, and father.

He loved Sister the best of all. Big tears formed in her eyes and she was unable to talk. "Sister, I know you do not understand right now. For a long time I have suffered because of a terrifying fear of death, but neither Buddha nor my family could help me. Now I have peace. You yourself can remember the times I prayed to the god of this and the god of that. My whole life has been nothing but fear! I was afraid of the dark, I was afraid of my own shadow, I was afraid of the toilet. Afraid of creaks and noises in the house, afraid of silence. I tell you, Sister, even if I had no more life, I could actually die in peace! I am free from all those fears. Can you understand that feeling? I could say I am ready to die, in fact. If you give me up because I have found the way to Jesus, then I have to say yes, I will go out from Father's house."

Her lips trembled and she sat near his side throughout the day.

Yonggi loved his heritage. He would always honor his grandfather and his father—not with incense and superstition, but with the tales of their past which he would someday tell to his children and grandchildren. He would focus on the lives they lived and the ideas they handed down, on the good they stood for. But he could never bow to their tomb nor talk to their dead spirit. God demanded total loyalty to Jesus and would tolerate no resemblance of worship toward any other. He had read the Bible only in bits and pieces, but that much he could tell. The disciples forsook all and followed Him.

In the evening Father came to him and explained the verdict, the result of a family consultation that had been conducted without Elder Son. Saying he would no longer be partaker of the boy's life or death, he added what it was he had really come to say, that if Yonggi chose to talk about Christian things and to follow that foolish heresy, then he was no longer the son of Cho and was asked to leave the house.

"You go ahead and be a Christian if that's what you want to be, but be a Christian somewhere other than beneath my roof. And go on and be a good one while you're at it!"

No other word was spoken. Yonggi had not expected that degree of harshness even coming from Father. He had thought they might at least be glad that he was out of bed and walking. Their son was all but dead and now he was alive. And from today he was not their son.

Packing a few belongings in a white cloth bundle, Yonggi glanced about the room, then went to the outdated calendar, gently took it from the nail it hung upon and laid it on his empty bed. He stepped reluctantly into the night, trying hard to hold up his head. Walking briskly as if he had some place to go, he did in fact go directly to his uncle in the same city. His uncle had become a success—he even owned a refrigerator.

Standing at the bottom step, he called and soon the uncle appeared on the porch. "Unholy Christian, go away; ask your God to help you if you think He can."

He wheeled around as if struck by a force. Not Uncle, too! Had he and Father conspired against him? Bending forward in a sudden moment of nausea, he gripped hold of his stomach and walked back the way he had come. What had he done so terribly wrong? On the road back he stopped and stared down the narrow passageway that led to his house. How beautiful were the tiles on the roof and the comforts inside. Like a lonely dog, he watched in stillness in a glance that combined longing and fear. Though his body had little strength, he dared not stay until daylight, lest Father's familiar footsteps be the first to greet the morning.

"Father! Father!" he cried out in a frail voice, this time looking up to the heavens as he sobbed, tears rolling down his face and into his collar. *"Abaji! Abaji!"* ("Father, Father," in Korean, pronounced "ahh-ba-jee." Used to address one's earthly father, and in familiar speech, to address God when praying.)

His feet carried him far into the city, weary and spent, ready to drop before he reached the docks, all the while his mind mulling over one statement Jesus had said: "In my Father's house are many mansions. In my Father's house are many mansions. In my Father's house are many mansions. . ." (John 14:2).

5

The Truth Shall Make You Free
(1955-1956)

In Pusan he devised a plan and found a man at the docks to help him carry it out. The stench of the boats mingled with the smell of dead fish and human waste, and the breeze was just enough to make it omnipresent. The method he hit upon was not honorable, but he was determined to see it through. Cho knew a Korean man who was good at forgery; he could carry off almost any deception. For a price, he agreed to counterfeit a high school diploma issued in the name of Cho Yonggi. It would take a little time to make all the fancy designs and get the seals and stamps to look just right. But he agreed to have it ready in time for the entrance examination at the medical university.

His mind was made up. Nothing was going to stand in his way. He made every preparation he could think of and he read the dictionary without ceasing. He prayed to Hananim: "Please, please, I've got to make it. I've got to pass that examination."

Life so far had not been fair, he figured, and that justified all he was doing now. Anyway, it was an honorable profession to seek, and a service to mankind and to Korea.

One thing he overlooked. But it was too late. When the test results were announced, his photo appeared in the newspaper along with two other finalists. Yonggi Cho made the third highest score on the medical exam, among several hundred participants. Identified as a graduate of Pusan Technical High School and the son of Cho Doo Chun and Kim Bok Sun, the younger Cho might have made it except the newspaper reporter made a trip to congratulate the high school on graduating such an adept student and to gather more details and comments from the boy's teachers and school officials. His successful score got him in trouble. He was not even registered at Pusan Tech. When the truth was discovered, he was dismissed from med school no sooner than he had been admitted. A fake diploma turned into an expensive nightmare.

And a nightmare, it was. The one dream he had clung to was his ambition to be a medical doctor. Now he wakened in the night perspiring and crying at the same time. It was a recurring dream. He saw himself standing before the entrance to the medical university, pounding on the heavy iron gates, crying but to no avail.

The words from his childhood rang in his ears as if his father were speaking, "Do not look up at the tree you can never climb." But the tree cast its shadow, and Cho could neither run nor chop it down.

There was one other way.

In Korea there was a shortage of doctors and the rules allowed two ways to enter the profession. One was to study at the medical university. The other was to train in a hospital, though at the end such a one could never reach the standing of the doctors who graduated from med school.

Accepted on a trial basis at a hospital in Pusan, Cho wrapped bandages and washed pots, emptied ashtrays and read thermometers. By gaining the doctor's approval, he was fast promoted to dressing wounds and giving shots. He enjoyed the white overcoat and in time the blood splotches at the end of a day began to make him feel he was a real doctor. At night he was permitted to read the doctor's medical books. With dormitory facilities, meager and cramped though they were, he entered the work-study program with full determination and all the vigor his body would allow. He even found the hospital smell of cresol to be pleasant, a reminder of his old dream to be a medical doctor.

Dysentery was one of the most common sicknesses among babies. Due to a shortage of fertilizer, human excrement was used on the fields to make the crops grow. The mothers often gave babies who were teething a raw eggplant or cucumber to chew on even though it had been grown on land fertilized in this manner. Hence, so much dysentery.

Among the common people, sickness was largely attributed to evil spirits. Therefore many tried the *Chim* doctors before coming to the clinic. In one case, out of desperation a small child was brought in, her side swollen and bruised and terribly painful at the slightest touch. When Cho lifted the child's dress to examine her, she screamed in fear. The supervising doctor looked on and reproached the mother for having taken the child to a Chim doctor.

"These black speckles and bruises are where the Chim doctor has stuck needles into her side," he pointed out knowingly, though the mother denied it all along.

The belief that evil spirits caused illness was the basis for stabbing hot needles into an afflicted part to kill the evil spirit supposed to have caused the problem. Sometimes coins were heated and pressed into the flesh with similar reasoning. Many old people had incredible scars on their backs and arms.

This child had over twenty black specks on her side where she had been stabbed with a needle. When the doctor required surgery, the mother would not allow it. She feared that to cut the child would let more evil spirits get inside to kill her.

Another treatment in use at that time was the "flesh cure." An old Korean "doctor" might sell a bite of bear lung and guarantee improved breathing, adding that if the patient did not get better he would refund half the fee. The idea behind the flesh cures was that the meat of certain animals was thought to be good for certain ailments. The part of the animal corresponding to the ailing part of the person was fed to the sick person. Meat from deer, wild boars, tigers, bears, cattle, hogs, lizards, dogs, fish, cats, and snakes was supposed to carry specific healing properties. Sometimes healthy people ate from the various organs of one of these animals to insure staying well. A few individuals went out once a year to get a live lizard to swallow so that their legs would be strong.

Similarly herbs have been used throughout Korea, the

shape of the plant or its fruit determining its best function in relation to human health. As herbs are close to "modern" medicine, they continue to be used widely in the East right along with Western medicine. The danger of herbs is the poor diagnosis of a disease and improper dosage of the herb. Also the herb doctor might have given a little to stimulate the heart, then the patient would take a lot, reasoning that if a little was good, more must be better.

Certain rules had to be observed in the preparation of herbs. They were never to be cooked in utensils made of metal but rather in clay containers, clay having the nearest likeness to the constituents of the human body. For cutting the plants no metal knife could be used, but only bamboo-sharpened tools were considered appropriate.

Orange peels were used as sedatives, and the willow for rheumatism. Dandelions were good for stomachaches, and for boils and abscesses.

Honey was used as a cohesive agent in the preparation of pills.

While watermelons had some value in soothing a sore throat, they were considered the main cause of the spread of typhus epidemics in China. On the advice of a European bacteriologist, an edict was issued to forbid the sale of sliced or cut watermelon in China, and the precaution found its way to Korea. People learned to get into the habit of pouring scalding water over the melons before cutting through them to avoid carrying disease from the rind to the knife.

Confucius had said, "If, while being a student of the

past, a man also understands the new things which surround us, he may be used as a teacher." Korean medical books contained the wisdom of the East and the discoveries of the West. Even the war contributed to the nation's medical knowledge.

Cho was determined to learn. Yet the work was not easy and he began to grow fatigued before each morning's routine was finished. From early morning until late at night he lost himself in the human suffering that was constantly flooding the hallways and moaning in the night. Yet he studied the books which the doctors willingly loaned him.

Oriental medicine involved much more than the hundreds of acupuncture points; it involved a whole philosophy of the total man. Nor was the use of herbs merely folk medicine. When East and West began to merge, for instance, it was seen that "Chinese horsetail," used by the Koreans in treating asthma, turned out to be a major source of natural ephedrine, a current Western remedy for asthmatic conditions.

Man is a summary of the universe, it was taught, a small world, though complete, in relation to the larger world. Being an integral part of the whole, and at the same time a miniature version of it, he is subject to the same universal laws. Hence, there was much talk of balance in Eastern medicine. Prolonged straining of the eyes was harmful to the blood and the heart. Prolonged lying in bed was harmful to respiration and to the lungs, so breathing exercises were designed for the patients. Prolonged sitting was harmful to the flesh and spine. Prolonged standing, harmful to bones and the kidneys;

and prolonged walking, harmful to the muscles and liver.

Certain organs of the body were solids, while others were sacs, and each had a direct influence on another. A great amount of time was spent studying the pulses, for it was believed that every organ in the body, not just the heart, had its own pulse; and the strength and quality of the pulses determined how perfectly or imperfectly the organ was functioning. It took years of experience to be proficient in reading the many pulses; doctors were usually sons of doctors, growing up in a continual environment of training. But war had taken its far-reaching toll in Korea and there was a need to turn more and more to foreign medicine for faster results in combating the diseases brought on by filth and poverty in an overpopulated city.

Cho's own body lacked the strength and health necessary to keep going. Every day the clinic was full, nor was there room in the hospital wards for any more. When people were sick, they smelled of the sickness.

Yet he pored over the medical books in the night. Medicines for ailments above the chest should be taken after meals. Medicines for ailments below the heart and stomach should be taken before meals. Medicines for sickness in the four limbs should be taken early in the morning on an empty stomach; and for afflictions of bones and marrow, in the evening after a meal.

Liquid medications served to cleanse the intestines, to stimulate the blood circulation and to restore the balance between Um and Yang. Pills were used for alleviating congestions, and powders were taken for stomach and intestinal afflictions. There was much to learn. He wished his own body would cooperate and not tire out so, and he longed for more time to study.

Concentrating on modern medicine now, he was writing prescriptions, alleviating needless pain wherever possible. The staff doctors recognized that Cho was a rapid learner who seemed capable of accurate diagnoses while at the same time giving careful consideration to the total patient. Here seemed to be a young intern who was a part of all he ever met, hungry to absorb learning from whatever direction it came; yet personable and gentle with every suffering individual, he reached out to each one if not with hope, then with kindness. His youth itself might have indeed been his greatest drawback to the gaining of a patient's confidence, wisdom somehow being associated with age. Truly at nineteen he was "Doctor Cho," though as yet he did not have that licensing piece of paper.

As if fascinated by every new medication that came out, he read the latest journals and labeled every sample tube or bottle indelibly in his mind. It was the human body itself, however, that drew his greatest study time. Cho studied the healthy body perhaps more than he studied disease, compelled to know what was expected of the body and how it was designed to function. The least idle moment would catch him sketching a cell tissue and all its parts, through every chromosome change and cell division to the growth of a new cell.

In his pockets he carried diagrams of leg muscle expansions and contractions, of blood circulation through veins and capillaries, and drawings of livers and lungs, hearts and stomachs. Yet he often wore the look of a daydreamer and scribbled poetry on scratch pads. Over doodles of biceps and nerve centers, he had written a part of Hamlet's soliloquy from Shakespeare: "What a piece of work is a man! How noble in reason! how infinite in faculty! in form and moving, how express and admirable! . . And yet, to me, what is this quintessence of dust?"[13]

Beside his study table he had taped a famous poem written by John Donne in seventeenth century Europe: "No man is an island, entire of itself; every man is a piece of the continent, a part of the main; if a clod be washed away by the sea, Europe is the less, as well as if a promontory were, as well as if a manor of thy friends or of thine own were; any man's death diminishes me, because I am involved in mankind; and therefore never send to know for whom the bell tolls; it tolls for thee."[14]

When he was nineteen, Yonggi was called to the farmhouse at Eonyang. Grandfather was ninety years old and he had completed his turn at things and his body lay at the mercy of his three sons and one daughter. Grandfather was dead. He had earlier been a landowner and his funeral was sizable. The large, blue tent made a bright, colorful array in front of the house where the many people gathered before proceeding to the cemetery below the peach orchard. True to custom, someone sprinkled coins into the field and he was laid into the ground. Standing tall and stiff at the head of the coffin, Yonggi Cho, favorite grandson, looked upon the body and did something that the whole family was never to forget—he fainted. He did not mean to faint; he certainly did not want to faint. He confessed later that he was concerned for the condition of his own body and, wanting desperately to live, he was gripped by fatalistic thoughts on the power of death, even his own death.

In the spring "Doctor Cho" began coughing a lot and lost weight again. He lost the zeal he had once demonstrated. He returned to the farmhouse to recuperate. While he was sick his closest brother, Yong Ou, now fifteen, spent part of his high-school vacation at Eonyang. "Tell me how to get the power of concentration, how to help myself," Yonggi probed his younger brother's face for a way to health. Speaking in jest, but keeping a straight face, Yong Ou advised his elder brother to take a brimful cup of water and run with it around the field without spilling it, saying that he could overcome in that way. Yonggi tried it.

By now he thought he must have been destined to sickness. Yet whenever he read his own palm it seemed he was to marry and father a family and that his life was to count for something important to the world.

Too weak to walk down to the village where a fair took place every five days, he asked Grandmother to go and buy some books for him to read. He told her to purchase whatever the fair had available, anything she could find for him to read. Although she was uneducated and almost illiterate herself, she selected Hermann Hesse's books in Korean. Yonggi was baffled that a grandmother could pick up just the right books for the right moment. The German novelist, who had won the Nobel prize for literature in 1946, spoke to Cho's mind as he too searched for self-realization and the meaning of life. He envied the youthful character in one of the books who seemed suddenly to come alive inwardly.

Hesse had described Cho in that moment:

Like a young plant hitherto quietly and intermittently developing which suddenly begins to breathe
harder and to grow, as though in a miraculous hour
it has become aware of the law which shapes it and
begins to strive toward the fufillment of its being,
the boy . . . began rapidly and eagerly to gather and
tauten his energies. He felt changed, growing; he
felt new tensions and new harmonies between
himself and the world. There were times, now, in
music, in Latin, and mathematics, when he could
master tasks that were still far beyond his age and the
scope of his schoolmates. Sometimes he felt capable
of any achievements. At other times he might forget
everything and daydream with a new softness and
surrender, listen to the wind or the rain, gaze into
the chalice of a flower or the moving waters of the
river, understanding nothing, divining everything,
lost in sympathy, curiosity, the craving to comprehend, carried away from his own self toward
another, toward the world, toward the mystery and
sacrament, the at once painful and lovely disporting
of the world of appearances. Thus, beginning from
within and growing toward the meeting and
confirmation of self and world. . . .[15]

Yonggi read the books as if reading for the first time
his own mind, his hopes, his dreams. If only his body
would cooperate.

A younger brother was permitted a visit to the country

while Yonggi was "acting strangely," as the family had phrased it. The last two babies had been boys, born during the Korean War. Neither of them knew the life at Eonyang nor were they around their brother long at a time, if indeed he was to be called their kin at all.

Five-year-old Yong Chan admired Elder Brother as if some distant hero. Having been told not to bother him, he tried to spin his top as long as possible, a game to challenge himself alone if need be. But it was great delight to glance up at times and find Elder Brother watching him, and greater still if he seemed to be smiling. Top-spinning sometimes spun you with it, losing yourself for a moment in the movement of colors running together as one. Yong Chan was much more skillful at the long-spin than his tall paragon.

He loved to hear his brother laugh; it seemed to be a signal to show when he was serious or joking. Elder brothers were supposed to look dignified and serious in front of their siblings. There were times, though, when Yong Chan was taken in by his pranks. When Yong Chan asked him how to catch a baby bird and what it felt like, Yonggi told him to find a small fuzzy peach that was just a nub, green and firm, and to keep it warm in his pocket and it would one day turn into a beautiful baby bird. Though he did as instructed, the green peach remained a hard, green peach, no matter how caressingly he stroked it.

Unable to read all of the finger-writings in the soot on the kitchen wall, Yong Chan begged Brother to read them. Grandmother laughed every time, shaking her head and throwing up her arms. Yonggi had drawn his

finger through the oil-blackened soot, scribbling prophetic things about his future:

"I will receive a doctorate degree by the time I am
thirty."

"I will travel around the world as a young man."

"I will receive the Nobel prize someday."

All the brothers and sisters laughed when they heard
these strange ideas, but the family let it go on because
everyone thought he was going to die and he may as well
be tolerated for all his idiosyncrasies. He had always been
peculiar and sick. And anyway the doctor had said he
would die.

Whether at the farmhouse to recuperate and clear up
soiled lungs or at the hospital dormitory to keep on
trying, Yonggi battled with a constant struggle between
his mind and his body, between what he wanted to do and
what he could not do. Refreshed by the memory and
companionship of his young admirer for those few days
at Eonyang, he returned to the hospital work-study
program. A new thought intruded on him which he was
unable to formulate into a scientific logic—the thought
that love radiated some sort of healing power. It didn't
make sense, but that little brother whom he had hardly
known had had as much effect on his condition as
Hermann Hesse had on his mind.

Hesse had written that every healthy person must
have a goal in life and that life must have content.[16]
That's why Yonggi had written crazy ambitions on the
kitchen wall. Hesse said that if a person were to
concentrate all his will power on a certain end, he would
be able to achieve it. Yonggi wanted to be healthy, so

if he aimed beyond health, he would surely make it. The books had spoken directly to him: "You can achieve anything if you desire passionately enough."[17]

He figured this principle must work the other way too. Vaguely he remembered reading a sentence in the Bible that said of man, "As he thinketh in his heart, so is he" (Prov. 23:7).

Was it possible that his sickness could be related to his constantly seeing sickness at the hospital? Hadn't his high-school biology teacher shown them some weird specimens of damaged lungs and what-have-you which he had kept in formaldehyde? And when the teacher had lectured on tuberculosis he had distinctly said that the disease occurs more frequently in men than women and especially that tall men with long, slender necks were susceptible to TB. Yonggi had looked about the classroom and frightfully discovered he had the longest neck in the room. At home he looked into the mirror, afraid that because he had a long neck then he would contract TB. Had it not been so? How much power might the mind exercise over the body and other matter?

In a matter of weeks he again lacked exuberance for the medical work or anything else; he grew depressed and began to take long evening walks. The crowded dormitory life was in no way conducive to lifting his spirits. One evening as he walked, his feet wandered into the YWCA, where an American ex-marine stood lecturing. Cho guessed that he was preaching, though he had never heard a sermon. When the young man finished, through his Korean interpreter he called to the front any who wanted to know Jesus or who wanted to rededicate their lives to God. Without hesitation, Cho walked boldly to the front.

"What do you want?" the young preacher asked.

"Both," replied Cho. "I want to know Jesus and I want to rededicate my life to God."

Many foreign evangelists to Korea have returned to their home countries with impressive numbers to claim as "new converts," though the wording of their question in the altar invitation may have carried an entirely different nuance to the hearers. In Korea, anyone who already knew Jesus nevertheless wanted to keep knowing Him, if not to know more of Him. Hence, the whole audience might go forward, even though they might have been long-standing elders and deacons in the church and perhaps "know Jesus" as well as the visiting speaker did.

For Cho, however, this was the first time he could listen to another man pray with him. He had tried to pray only a few times in the dorm, hardly getting past "Father, Father," before a roommate would barge in to find him talking to the Unseen.

For the first time he could have it outlined to him; he could discover just what he needed to do in order to establish communication with Jesus. As important as it was for him to accept Jesus, he decided it was even more urgent that Jesus accept him. That was the crux of the matter. And it seemed to be the major difference between the teachings of Christ and all the other religions of mankind. On religion, Cho was an expert. So much were the Buddhist sutras a part of him that he could have been a monk. In Buddhism, as well as all the others, man was striving to be good enough to merit God's approval; hence, individuals everywhere lived in dread and fear of the wrath of a God they did not know. In truth, no man could ever measure up to the perfection of God and His holiness—no matter how great the sums of money he might give to charity nor how many orphans he might support. God himself took all the competition out of it by simply showing that no man is perfect but that all have sinned and come short of the glory of God. God himself provided the only way whereby man might be saved from his own path to destruction. That is, He sent His Son, Jesus, to take on all of the wrath of God himself for us, thus making everyone equal and giving everyone an equal chance, regardless even of the degrees of bad in the deeds of men. The only thing left for man to do was to give up trying on his own merits and confess his sins to Jesus. That is what the Bible said: A-B-C—Ask, Believe, Confess. Ask Jesus to forgive me, believe that He has, and confess Him as Lord and Master of my life in all I say and do. The Bible said that every person must be "born again"—born not only of water, as in the birth from the womb of woman, but that all persons must be born also of the Spirit.

Not until the individual takes the first step and acts on one thing he understands, can he begin to participate in the next steps. Some people say they want to understand the whole Bible before they do anything about securing eternal life for their souls. It does not work that way; it is one of the principles of faith, one of the principles of God, that a person grows in his knowledge of God only one step at a time and unless he actually takes those steps can he ever graduate to the next ones. Knowing them is not enough.

Cho thought it was the same as the weaving he had once observed when an old man sat at a loom threading one strand at a time. In the weaver's mind there was a picture of the ultimate design he was creating, and to skip one color or to substitute another was to miss the design altogether.

Man must never take God and weave a religion around Him, he thought, binding Him by the limitations of man. Man must yield to God instead and let God weave him into a more perfect whole.

Perhaps that was why the Bible used the term "born again." Just as an unborn baby cannot eat or think as a teen-ager, neither can one who is spiritually unborn handle the light of the total Scriptures. He only thinks he can. Give a flashlight to a baby and he thinks he is using it wisely, merely burning the batteries. It requires a growth process as well as a birth process. The ways of God are as orderly as the functions of the human body, requiring elimination of sin even as the body requires elimination of waste matter. Both the physical and the spiritual require food. Is that what the Bible meant, saying that man does not live by bread alone, but by every word that proceeds from the mouth of God? In more ways than he could grasp at once, Cho thought that the human body and the spiritual life ran parallel, for even the Scriptures constantly compared the two.

"Would you like to meet a missionary?" asked the ex-marine. "I would like to introduce you to a friend of mine who pastors a mission church near here and prays for the sick."

The next Sunday he was free from duties at the

hospital, so Yonggi attended church at the World Mission in Pusan. Everybody in the room seemed to be singing. He could sing along with them if he wanted to, or he could just keep quiet if he chose. He had been afraid of church but now it seemed to be a sort of incubator where the friendly atmosphere provided warmth. Anybody could come, even if he was not a member, and dues were not required. A preacher talked through an interpreter, explaining some characteristics about God, but he was not wearing long black robes as the Buddhist priests did. As before, when the speech was over and the preacher invited anyone to come up and talk privately, Cho stepped to the front and shook hands with the missionary. Later introducing himself as the Reverend Louis P. Richards, he invited Cho to a small office inside the church.

Here, for the first time, Cho made sure of his own relationship to God, for then and eternity. "Father, Father!" he closed his eyes and started to pray. "This is Cho Yonggi. For a long time I have accepted your Son, Jesus. But from today I want to ask you to also accept me. I see that we, as imperfect human beings, cannot come to you in our own ways, because you are the God of the universe. Just as the Korean government has its own requirements for issuing a medical license, I see you have your own ways for us to get a passport to your country. So I tell you, from today I want to be sure I am filling out the papers your way and not just my own way. If I understand it right, I can borrow Jesus' name and ask you to forgive me. Father, that is what I am doing now. Please forgive me for ever calling on some other gods; please forgive me for stealing coal from the American Navy for cooking fuel; please forgive my obstinacy and curses directed at that poor, beautiful girl who brought me this Bible I have in my hand; I'm sorry for the times I have cheated and lied, Lord, and I wish I could promise you I would never do those things again; but you know I am only a human being. I will try, Father. But even though I see I can be a Christian, I know I can never be perfect. So I really thank you for loving me and sending your own Son to take my punishment which I'm sure I could not endure. But I will be to you a son and honor your name. So I ask you to give me a chance and to teach me day by day how to be more and more like Jesus. Thank you. In Jesus' name I pray like Pastor Richards taught me. Amen."

"Doctor Cho" had a relapse of TB. For over two full years he had done fairly well, his body standing up to the strenuous work-study program. A little longer and he would earn his own license. Only God knew how desperately he had wanted to be a medical doctor!

When his cough continued to worsen Cho asked a staff doctor to examine him and together they viewed the x-rays. Why? Why must he constantly live in the monstrous shadow of TB? What good was his praying, wanting to be like Jesus? He was sure God's Son did not have TB.

With the recurrence of the disease, he had to leave his studies unfinished. Even streptomycin, which had been used for only a decade in other parts of the world, required the help of rest and sunshine, two things an intern could hardly afford.

TB had taken its toll the world over, and in Korea there was no way of knowing how many thousands carried the disease and how many went off to the mountains to die. Other cases were seldom fatal except when left hopelessly unattended.

The youthful ex-marine, Kenneth Tice, made a room for Cho, and Mrs. Richards invited him to their home for the main meal every day. "Pastor Richards, we are not related, so how can you and your wife keep on feeding me this good food as though you love me?" Cho asked one day.

"Because Jesus saved us too," came the reply. "One world, one household."

Confucian society regarded itself a large family with five basic vertical relationships: ruler-subject, father-son, husband-wife, elder-younger, and friend to friend. If these relationships were in order, then a proper horizontal family could exist without chaos in the world. Now in the Christian society, there was also one big family. That seemed to be why every Christian was out trying to find his brothers throughout the world.

Little by little, Cho began to see the relevance of what he read: "God sent forth his Son, made of a woman, made under the law, To redeem them that were under the law, that we might receive the adoption of sons. And because ye are sons, God hath sent forth the Spirit of his Son into your hearts, crying Abba, Father. Wherefore thou art no more a servant, but a son; and if a son, then an heir of God through Christ" (Gal. 4:4-7).

Cho came to be the preacher's interpreter, Pastor Richards teaching him from the Bible and from experiences with life. "The Word of God has tremendous creative power. It will recreate your lungs, it will heal you." Cho memorized all he heard and read.

One day he was ready to put it to a test. He locked the door of his room and began to pray. "Mister Jesus," he spoke out, "I want to meet you and have a consultation about my future." He waited. Nothing happened.

He did not know this was not the way to try the teachings of God. He did not know the real way to try the teachings of God was to put them in practice every day at work, at school, in the neighborhood. He did not know a medical doctor in the United States was to write a book in which he would state, "The sincere acceptance of the principles and teachings of Christ with respect to the life of mental peace and joy, the life of unselfish thought and clean living, would at once wipe out more than half the difficulties, diseases, and sorrows of the human race."[18]

He did not know forgiveness could eliminate headaches nor did he know clinging to grudges could cause them. He did not know doctors everywhere were concluding that hatred, pent-up anger, fear, jealousy, resentment, envy were responsible for perhaps 60 percent or more of the illnesses of man. He did not know one of the most powerful prayers a man could utter is, "Create in me a clean heart, O God; and renew a right spirit within me" (Ps. 51:10).

Cho shut his eyes tightly as if to induce a picture of Jesus. No vision appeared. He prayed all day, and by nighttime he was soaked in perspiration. Finally, drained and exhausted, his body gave in to sleep.

He awoke after midnight hungry from not having

eaten all day. "Okay, Mister Jesus, I'm ready to pray some more," he continued his prayer in the most polite way he knew to address the Savior. "Sir, I am quite hungry and it's late at night; if you can recreate my lungs then you must also be able to supply some noodles to soothe the hunger pains in my stomach." Continuing with his eyes closed and trying to remember everything he had been taught about prayer, Cho was startled to hear a loud knock on his door. Clad in a white smock and white hat, a delivery boy handed him a red and gold lacquer box from the nearby Chinese restaurant. "I saw your light on," the boy shrugged, "and I had one too many on my last run."

The boy must have wondered why Cho stared into his face so long and did not say a word.

Slurping the noodles and enjoying the side dish of *kimchi* that came together in the lacquerware, Cho was well awake by now. He finished and laid the wooden chopsticks across the dish in silence.

A neophyte at praying, he wondered why he had awakened at that exact moment. Suddenly a smell of smoke filled the air and to his left a cloud of gray smoke bellowed before him. In the same instant a fireman appeared in the room. Hadn't he locked the door after the delivery boy? He distinctly remembered locking it! All of this in a split second—the smoke, the fireman, his own flashbacks. But the fireman stood barefooted on the floor, a white robe draping his ankles. As quickly as it all happened, Cho glanced upward and his eyes fixed on the face of a man who looked straight into his eyes. From a wound on His forehead there oozed a stain of blood and a wreath of thorns sat upon His head. "My Lord! My Lord!"

The silence was broken by words from Cho's own lips.

Kneeling to Cho's level, the man pointed a finger at Cho and started talking clearly and distinctly: "Young man," he said, "you are ambitious. You are looking for fame and money. I tell you everything of this kingdom will crumble. But I have a kingdom that will not crumble. You are to go and preach about my kingdom that does not crumble."

Cho reached out as if to touch his visitor's garment. But he gently fell asleep and he did not awaken until morning.

In the morning there was no appearance of anyone but himself in the room nor any evidence of disturbance. There was nothing but the empty lacquer box with chopsticks lying respectfully across the edges. He himself felt rested, and as he stretched he said aloud, "Thank you, Lord, for a beautiful day today. . . ." His tongue uttered sounds he had never heard before but it felt good to release the wonderful bubbling inside him; he stopped and started again just to see whether he could. The "words" poured out with such euphony, sometimes repeating themselves but tumbling rapidly one behind the other. In what seemed only moments, the morning had passed. Cho had been intermittently singing and vocalizing his new sounds. His chest contained a strange warmth which seemed to make breathing easier.

With a spring in his gait, he walked outside. Seeing a group of young people sitting at a street vendor's stall, he eased up close and announced what he had heard: "There is a kingdom that does not crumble."

Over and over he collared one at a time to tell them,

"Jesus Christ has a kingdom that does not crumble.

"Korea has crumbled before—not once but many times. I know a kingdom that does not crumble, and it's not America, not Japan, not Russia, not England, not even China. Would you like to hear what somebody told me?"

By evening he made it to the Richards' table, and in bits and pieces he told of the sounds in his new song, still curious and secretly hoping someone else might have had a similar joy, some gauge by which to measure his own sanity.

Lou Richards, outwardly serene, inwardly his heart pounding with excitement, opened the Bible to the book of *Acts,* chapter two, and began reading as Cho followed in his Korean Bible:

> And when the day of Pentecost had come, they were all together in one place. And suddenly there came from heaven a noise like a violent, rushing wind, and it filled the whole house where they were sitting. And there appeared to them tongues as of fire distributing themselves, and they rested on each one of them. And they were all filled with the Holy Spirit and began to speak with other tongues, as the Spirit was giving them utterance. (Acts 2:1-4 NAS)

After continuing on to read the whole chapter aloud, Richards briefly explained to Cho that it seemed clear he had spoken in tongues. But he added that Cho could not go around preaching unless he went to Bible school.

Plans were formulated and Cho was to enter the Full

Gospel Bible Institute in Seoul, a school sponsored by the Assemblies of God.

Had he dared to follow God in the first place, rather than cling stubbornly to his ambition for personal fame in the medical profession, he wondered whether he might have been spared the TB relapse. All through life he sort of knew that after all he had learned during those earlier days from that girl's Bible, he had broken a silent promise to God. Now he was given another chance. It was not wrong to become a doctor, but he could see that his motive had been wrong. And anyway, God had a plan that superseded his own.

If not to be a doctor, at least he was to get more education. He felt satisfied. It was fulfilling to enter a life of purpose and direction, to be freed from scheming and worrying about the future. To be freed from the peach orchard and from all it stood for. "Ye shall know the truth, and the truth shall make you free" (John 8:32).

Yonggi Cho's birthplace in the southeastern village of Eonyang, Korea.

Dr. Cho sits where his mother used to do the family wash, reminiscing about his childhood. His sermons are often full of natural illustrations from the grass and rocks, the hillsides and the ponds, to show deep truths about life.

Returning to visit Eonyang Elementary School. Today the president of the nation encourages his people by displaying slogans and mottoes. One reads: "Koreans! Love Korea!" The one just above the door says, "Study hard. Learn well."

Yonggi Cho, standing second from the left, was on the running team at Eonyang Elementary School.

As preparation for this book, Cho returns to his elementary school. He was surprisingly greeted by his own fifth and sixth grade teachers, who are presently the principal and vice-principal.

Returning to the peach orchard he grew to hate, Cho recalls his bitter youth when he felt condemned to sickness, fear and hatred of anything that threatened to keep him from having a better life.

Yonggi, the firstborn son, was to hold a special place in the household of his father and mother.

Grandfather and Grandmother were proud the gods had blessed them with a grandson, whose filial duty it would be to burn the incense before their altar someday.

The Cho family. Yonggi Cho is standing second from left.

The five brothers in the Cho family. Left to right standing are Yong Bae, Yong Chan, Yong Mok (pastor-in-charge during Dr. Cho's travels). Seated, Yong Ou and Dr. Yonggi Cho.

Yonggi Cho, age 22, and Jashil Choi, 43, graduate as classmates together, not knowing at that time that they were to go through life as son-in-law and mother-in-law, as well as pastor and associate.

Graduation day, a dream long cherished. Away with tuberculosis!

March 1, 1965. Yonggi Cho married Sung Hae Kim.

Memorial photo, including brothers and sisters with their families, at the sixtieth birthday of Yonggi Cho's father.

The sixtieth birthday of Doo Chun Cho, Dr. Cho's father. In Korea only three birthdays are celebrated with significance—a 100-day-old baby, a one-year-old baby, and the sixty-year-old adult. Throughout Asia advanced age carries great honor.

A recent photo of Dr. Cho's parents, Doo Chun Cho and Bok Sun Kim.

Tent church at Taejo Dong, slum area of Seoul in 1958.

The church in her second location, Sodaemoon (West Gate).

The women carried what they could, the men carried the bricks, and a church was built.

Building the church. Used to carrying baby brothers and sisters on their backs, the Koreans donned a wooden cane for support and strapped thirty bricks to their backs. The church moved forward, and with her the nation.

The church complex at Yoido including the dome-shaped main auditorium; World Mission Center on the right with offices, teaching facilities, library, TV recording studio, cafeteria, and guest rooms and dormitory accommodations for 500; apartment building housing over 60 families; educational building; and gymnasium on the left which allows 3,000 of the overflow congregation to sit on the floor and participate in the worship via closed-circuit TV.

Diluting the homemade wine with water, Women's Fellowship speedily but efficiently prepares over 400 trays of wine cups for the monthly Lord's Supper. The church has a wine cellar under the building, where a two-year supply of grapes in huge crocks make their own wine for the ceremonial remembrance of the blood of Jesus in whom they are one and by whom they are healed.

(Photo by K.S. Hong)

It takes a lot of bread to serve the Lord's Supper once a month to 100,000 members. Women of the church work faithfully behind the scenes preparing rice-bread and homemade wine for the communion service.

(Photo by K.S. Hong)

Between services on Sunday, one congregation flows out as the next one packs in. "Some of you, take turns," says Cho, "and alternate your Sundays—leave room for the newer Christians to get inside." Five services are held one after the other from early Sunday morning until night, to accommodate the near 100,000 members and visitors.

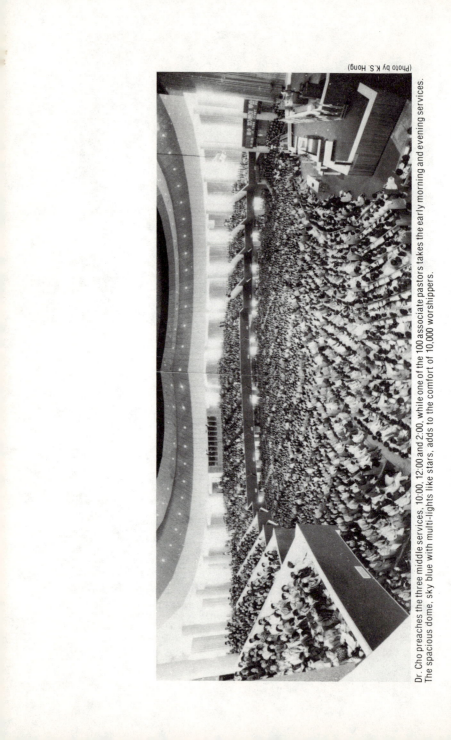

Dr. Cho preaches the three middle services, 10:00, 12:00 and 2:00, while one of the 100 associate pastors takes the early morning and evening services. The spacious dome, sky blue with multi-lights like stars, adds to the comfort of 10,000 worshippers.

Dr. Cho in his church office.

Every weekday morning the church-owned buses fan out to deliver the more than 100 pastoral assistants to house calls, Bible studies, prayer meetings, visits to the sick, and other ministries throughout the city.

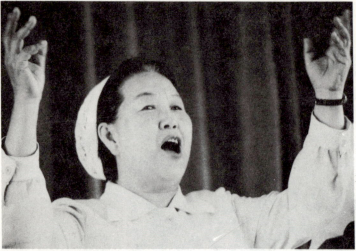

In her characteristically joyful manner, Jashil Choi leads the congregational singing.

(Photo by Nell Kennedy)

Jashil Choi leads the women of Korea to pray for the nations of the world, for "God has chosen the weak things of the world to confound the things which are mighty" (1 Cor. 1:27).

(Photo by Nell Kennedy)

Prayer Mountain.

(Photo by Neil Kennedy)

(Photo by Neil Kennedy)

On any day of the week at least a thousand people gather for fasting and prayer in the chapel at Prayer Mountain, praising God and expecting miracles. Many Korean Christians take a week or more of their annual vacation time in prayer and fasting at the mountain.

할수 있거든이 무슨 말이나 믿는 자에게는 능치 못함이 없느니라
IF YOU CAN! ALL THINGS ARE POSSIBLE TO HIM WHO BELIEVES

(Photo by Neil Kennedy)

A huge billboard at Prayer Mountain proclaims the truth of Mark 9:23.

Bringing tithes and offerings to the altar requires over seventy laborers, both men and women.

Balcony steps serve as pews when there is no other room to sit.

Always outgrowing herself, Full Gospel Central Church, on Yoido, seems never to be quite finished.

(Photo by Nell Kennedy)

Mrs. Cho directing the orchestra and choir in a Sunday service.

Hee Jae, their firstborn son.

With her husband traveling six months of the year, Mrs. Cho keeps in touch by phone. She serves as director of the publications department and also heads the school which the church operates.

Dr. Cho lectures on the principles of success at the World Mission Center, one of more than twenty church growth seminars conducted every year.

(Photo by Neil Kennedy)

Rev. Dr. Yonggi Cho.

(Photo by K.S. Hong)

Left to Right: Samuel, Dr. Cho, Hee Jae, wife Sung Hae, Sung Jae.

(Photo by K.S. Hong)

Dr. Cho serving as interpreter for his personal friend and guest speaker, Dr. Robert Schuller from the U.S.

(Photo by K.S. Hong)

Dr. Cho and Dr. John Hurston. Dr. Hurston serves as vice-president and dean of Church Growth International and has worked closely with Cho through the years.

6

Run, North Korean, Run

(1956-1958)

The first year went fairly smoothly and he studied insatiably, having free access to all the books on the shelves. But the Bible school had only started three years earlier, and its library was limited. He did not see why such an easy curriculum was spread over a two-year course when he could have completed it in one year.

Quickly he became Professor John Stetz's interpreter and was elected chairman of the student body. Like the other students, he did not always perform to his full capacity. One of the teachers often reprimanded them for their lazy study habits, calling them ping-pong preachers because they spent most of their free time at the ping-pong table in the recreation room.

"Memorize the Scriptures," the teacher told them. "There's more to it than merely getting through a course. Get hold of Hebrew; don't just pass a test and forget it the next day. Study what you think you know."

In the small class of '58 there was one student too zealous for the others to quite enjoy. For one thing, she was a woman, an older woman at that. One year younger than Cho's mother, this Mrs. Jashil Choi (pronounced "Chay" in Korean) had passed the school entrance exam by the skin of her teeth and had become a freshman at age forty-one. Whatever memory work was assigned, she was always the first to raise a hand and repeat the entire passage with perfect recollection. Never missing a word she was constantly being praised by the teacher. Her fellow-classmates hated it whenever the teacher used her as an example for them to follow. She would have been an object of jest to them had they not been in Bible school and felt compelled not to be unkind.

Another factor restrained them—she was rich. The regular students lived in the dormitory, cold and damp, while she owned a black car and hired a private driver. She was richly dressed.

Who was she anyway, and why had she come?

As chairman of the student body, Cho was approached by the others in the class to speak to her about not intimidating them, to coax her to make mistakes sometimes and fail to do her homework, at least now and then. "You are making a fool of us by always saying perfect memory work and boldly being first to raise your hand. Don't be such a good student, for our sakes," he urged her.

She had secretly looked up to him, admiring his example and striving continually to keep up with him and measure up in some small way to his abilities, the straight and tall Cho who assisted the missionary. The student body president, he was a zealous worker, not a bit bashful, always in the forefront where the action was; he had been a real inspiration to her since the day of the entrance exam. What was it he was asking her to do? Not to study? She had come here to study.

But the next morning when the professor called on the class, she held back. When no one in the whole class answered, she seemed to see the teacher's face pale with disappointment. His will to teach seemed to lose its spark. She couldn't help herself—up shot her hand and she recited the memory work. If anything, she started to study harder. She could see in Professor Stetz both zeal and sincerity. He was trying to make sure they had a firm foundation, layer on layer, week after week building on the previous week's learning. He was trying to help them transfer their concepts and apply their learning. Learning was useful. This was different from the usual Korean approach to learning, where studying was for the purpose of passing the test. She would do it the Stetz way!

In her youth, money had been the most precious thing in the world to her; now it was time. She began coming to school by streetcar and while riding to and from school she used the time to memorize Bible verses or to pray. At times, she became so engrossed with her devotions that she would miss her stop. Time and again she rode to the end of the line before realizing it. The conductor was kind. "Well, old student, you did it again. Now on your way back, would you please watch for your stop?"

Learning was a struggle for her. She never forgot praying her way through the entrance examination. She felt certain she had failed it, so she spent the rest of the day in chapel after the test, praying, "Oh, Hananim, just let me pass. Just let me in. I know there must be thousands of women who are in the same predicament I was in before, on their way to destruction. I've got to warn them. So I've got to get into Bible school."

Hours later when the test results were posted, she had slipped up to search for her name among those who scored successfully. Starting at the bottom of the list, her eyes daring not to glance too far up, she squinted to verify what she saw. "Hallelujah!" she shouted. "Oh, hallelujah!" She danced up and down, clapping her hands and waving both arms like a cheerleader. Her name was there, at the very bottom of the list. "Hallelujah! Hallelujah!"

Out of curiosity she then peered to see who had made the top score. Cho Yonggi, whoever that was.

"The only reason I didn't envy him was because we were on the same team," she confessed later. Being chairman of evangelism, Mrs. Choi encouraged the young highbrow to speak out in street services and she let him be the leader. To her, he seemed so eloquent, so bold and graceful. What she herself lacked in public speaking ability, she tried to make up for through prayer and fasting. When the several students on her team went out for street meetings she was so much a part of the team that when Yonggi preached fearlessly, she was glad; it seemed as though her other self was doing it. She recognized how psychologically she was compensating for her own inability to speak before a crowd.

With the money he earned interpreting and translating for the missionaries, Cho bought a bass drum for the outdoor meetings. On occasions he treated the entire team to lunch away from the school; it felt so good to be their benefactor. Though it might take weeks or months to jingle enough money in his pocket to treat them again, he loved the taste of chivalry. They had all passed through the Communist war less than four years ago, so the simplest treat was a treat indeed. Sensitive to Yonggi's need for leadership opportunities, Mrs. Choi refrained her hand from picking up the tab and joined in the simple joys of the meager outings.

They made a good team. It was their routine to take the streetcar from the school to the park to conduct their meetings, except when an unpleasant streetcar conductor would not permit Yonggi to get on with the huge bass drum. If one had to walk, they all walked, singing along the way, as Yonggi beat the drum to the tempo of the melody. It was amusing in light of the Chinese meaning for Yonggi —"the drummer" or "bell ringer." Was he not, after all, fulfilling the name his father had given him?

Still no one really knew their classmate and team leader, Jashil Choi. No one dreamed or suspected that her teen-age daughter was destined some day to become Yonggi's wife, nor even knew, for that matter, that she had a daughter. She was simply the chairman of evangelism. There did not really seem such a wide gap in their ages any more. They somehow never thought of her as a married woman, the licensed nurse that she was, caring for a family at home. They did not know the life she had escaped from in North Korea. They could never be a part of the history she had lived, having been born August 15, 1915, just five years after all of Korea had become a police state under the Japanese.

Prison officials had brought a tortured man to die in the Provincial Hospital in Pyongyang, the important seaport city along the Taedong River. His front teeth missing and his face as pale as death, the man raised his eyelids to look at his wife and two children at his side. He looked a long time at his wife as if trying to sear her image into his mind for eternity, and then he gazed intently for some moments at his five-year-old daughter, Jashil, on whose back was strapped her baby brother, Song Min, in the traditional fashion. Though a child, she sensed that her father was leaving them, and confirmed her fears when she looked up in time to notice her mother brushing away silent tears with the back of her fingers. In a feeble voice the man managed to whisper to his child, whom he had hardly seen since she was born, "Why did you have to come into this awful place?"

She darted out of the room. Her whole being cried uncontrollably and loudly, as she ran about with Brother still asleep on her back. She never knew whether her father had meant the hospital or this world as "this awful place," but she grew to suspect he had meant the latter.

That was the last time she saw her father, as he died that night, the deepest commitments of his heart never realized. He had given his life to free Korea from Japanese rule, sacrificing months at a time away from his family to support an independence movement among Koreans living in China. Some Koreans in China sent a petition to the American minister in Peking, which read in part: "The Japanese have encouraged immorality by removing Korean marriage restrictions, and allowing marriages without formality and without regard for age. There have been marriages at as early an age as twelve. Since the annexation there have been 80,000 divorce cases in Korea. The Japanese encourage, as a source of revenue, the sale of Korean prostitutes in Chinese cities. Many of these prostitutes are only fourteen and fifteen years old. It is part of the Japanese policy of race extermination, by which they hope to destroy all Koreans. May God regard these facts."[19]

It was claimed the Japanese encouraged the sale of morphine and other hard drugs, the sale of which was banned in their own country, in order to demoralize the Koreans.

The year preceding the death of Jashil's father had stirred the nationals to patriotism and vexed the Japanese like smoke in a wasp's nest. The *Samil* Three-One Movement of 1919 (Three-One referring to March—the third month, the first day) had played havoc throughout the land. On the designated Saturday at 2:00 P.M., Korean patriots by the thousands had marched out of their homes and shops to gather in city parks and other prearranged centers everywhere to proclaim freedom. It was one of the most amazingly planned movements of its kind in modern history.

Spurred on by U.S. President Woodrow Wilson's "Fourteen Points" following World War I, Koreans had built their hopes around one sentence defining his proposal for a League of Nations: "To provide for the freedom of small nations, to prevent the domination of small nations by big ones."

Here was the clarion call to Korea. A Declaration of Independence was drawn up with thirty-three signers, fifteen of whom were Christians. Instructions were sent out calling for absolutely no violence, whereby the weak things would set themselves up to confound the strong:

"Do not insult the Japanese, do not throw stones, do not hit with your fists, for these are the acts of barbarians."

Each city had been mapped out in districts and thousands of copies of the Declaration of Independence circulated by school children and women. Every social strata of the community was united. Men of high rank stood with the coolies; shopkeepers closed their stores; policemen who had worked under the Japanese took off their uniforms and joined the crowds; porters and laborers, scholars and preachers, men, women, and children all came together. The Japanese people were not injured and the Japanese shops were left alone; when the police attacked, elders ordered the people to submit without resistance. It had been an unheard of demonstration.

The thirty-three signers chose martydom. On the morning of March 1, all but one of them (Rev. Kil was temporarily delayed in Pyongyang) met at the Blue Moon Restaurant in Seoul, where they had invited some prominent Japanese. After the last supper, so to speak, the Declaration was produced before their guests and read, then dispatched to the Governor-General. The signers telephoned the Central Police Station, informed the shocked officials what they had done, and added that they would wait in the restaurant until the police came to arrest them. Not only Seoul but the whole country had in a few minutes burst into open demonstration, crying *"Mansei! Mansei!* May Korea live ten thousand years." "Mansei" was the Korean pronunciation of the Chinese characters which the Japanese called *"Banzai,"* their victory cry for "Hoorah!"

The Declaration of Independence, written in the lofty tone of the ancient prophets, was the cry of New Asia, not only Korea, struggling to find its way out of oppression and medieval militarism into the promised land of liberty and peace:

We herewith proclaim the independence of Korea and the liberty of the Korean people. We tell it to the world in witness of the equality of all nations and we pass it on to our posterity as their inherent right.

We make this proclamation, having back of us 5,000 years of history, and 20,000,000 of a united loyal people. We take this step to insure to our children for all time to come, personal liberty in accord with the awakening consciousness of this new era. This is the clear leading of God, the moving principle of the present age, the whole human race's just claim. . . .

. . . if the defects of the past are to be rectified, if the agony of the present is to be unloosed, if the future oppression is to be avoided, if thought is to be set free, if right action is to be given a place, if we are to attain to any way of progress, if we are to deliver our children from the painful, shameful heritage, if we are to leave blessing and happiness intact for those who succeed us, the first of all necessary things is the clearcut independence of our people. . . .

A new era wakes before our eyes, the old world of force is gone, and the new world of righteousness and truth is here. . . ."[20]

The Japanese, civilians and military alike, were given carte blanche, unrestricted discretion, to use the sword and club freely on any Korean they suspected of being a demonstrator. The nightmare in Korea had just begun.

Politically the Three-One Movement did not bring freedom to Korea, but it gave birth to a new breed of youth who would fight on and stand for the things they believed in; though a generation of their elders might die in prison, they would live on in their offspring to inherit the future.

For weeks following the demonstration children refused to go to school; though the schools reopened, there were no pupils. In one large junior high school, the boys were implored to come for their graduation exercises, to receive their certificate. The boys yielded and the commencement exercises were begun, with a number of official and distinguished Japanese present. After the certificates were handed to each boy, a thirteen-year-old student came to the front to make the school speech of appreciation to their teachers and to the authorities. He bowed low and spoke polite Japanese appropriate to formal occasions. "I have only this now to say," he concluded, with a noticeable change of voice while straightening to his full height. "We beg one more thing of you," he added with his chin up. He plunged one hand into his robe and pulled out the Korean flag. It was a crime to possess this flag. Waving it, he cried out, "Give us back our country. May Korea live forever. Mansei!"

All the class jumped up from their seats. Each boy pulled out a flag from under his coat and waved it, calling, "Mansei! Mansei! Mansei!" They tore up their certifi-

cates in front of the horrified guests, threw them on the
ground, and trooped out.[21]

It was into that decade of passionate determination
and brute force that Jashil Choi was plunged as a
fatherless child, one among many. The Japanese police
patrolled all areas of the city, long swords sheathed at
their sides. In the Haeju Village, southeast of the Sooyang
Mountains in northern Korea, she attended elementary
school. Theirs was one of fifteen wood-frame houses
filled with red clay-like mud, the roof thatched with rice
straw. Cottonseed oil filled the lamp which burned at
night, and no other brightness added to their lives.

One night when there was no supper, she wandered
into the lettuce patch to pick a few leaves, rolled them
over bean paste and ate. Still hungry, she cried into her
mother's apron, "Mama, tell me, why do we have to
live?"

"Why? Well, later you must get married," her mother
answered softly. "After marriage you will become rich.
You will have a nice home and lots of meat for your
table."

"Then what?" the child demanded.

"Then, in the end you will die. Why in the world is a
small child like you so worried about the future?"

After the 1919 incident, the Christians were recognized
as ardent patriots, because half the signers of the
Declaration of Independence had been Christians. The
churches enjoyed a period of popularity. Korea had been
profoundly affected by World War I, 1914-1918.

In 1920, an evangelistic team of college students from
Pyongyang visited Pusan and Chengju, holding meetings

that were crowded to the doors. One meeting drew 1,250 adults admitted by tickets. Churches united to organize evangelistic campaigns throughout the district, and workers were trained in special sessions for counseling. Groups of converts met weekly in village centers, asking admission to church membership.

The nation's capital, Seoul, experienced an increase in its Christian population in 1927. Church people refer to these times as "revival," but the Korean church was not at all a wilted plant that could be revived. It could only grow and reproduce itself. Since a headstrong spiritual wind in North Korea in 1907, Pyongyang and other centers in the North had hardly gone a day without some special encounter with God. In one town the temples had been torn down and their tiles used to make the roof of the church. Since the turn of the century Christians had met for prayer before sunrise every morning, a practice that has continued without fail to this day.

In 1928 there was a new wave of church growth in Pyongyang, where the Choi mother lived with her two children. Like golden wheat tossing in rhythm to a spirit that moved unseen upon the prairie, the people hummed and sang, swaying their bodies in a gentle euphoria. Meeting in gymnasiums at night or in canvas tents, they came to worship God because they wanted to. In three weeks over two thousand newcomers professed faith in Christ and were added to the powerful array of singers. Two hundred students bound themselves in a covenant of prayer, Bible reading and witness, and this number soon doubled to four hundred. They met in fifteen groups every Sunday except the first month, when they gathered unitedly.

"Jashil! Jashil! Come this evening," a friend called to her one afternoon. "They've just put up a tent beside the church, and they are going to tell about God, the good Father."

"Good father?"

"No. God, the good Father!"

Jashil could not find room in the tent. Already there was no place to sit and grown-ups were standing all around the edges and crowding the entrance. She sneaked around the outside pegs and crawled under, right where the pulpit was standing. At first a little frightened, she glanced around but felt all right the moment she saw a kind-looking man smiling at her. He motioned for her to come on in and sit down on the front row. Everybody sat close together on the ground as it made more room and kept them warm.

After what seemed like a great amount of singing, the evangelist was introduced as Lee Song Bong, the very one who had waved for her to crawl on into the tent. "Dear people, listen to my words," he started in an earnest voice. "Have you ever given it a thought as to why you were created? Do you know the purpose for which God has placed you here on this earth?"

This was the very question plaguing her thoughts lately. She had no answer. Mother had no answer either, really.

"Was man created just to eat and enjoy good food? Hogs are regarded as the biggest eaters. They eat and eat and never seem to be satisfied. They get so big and fat they can hardly walk. But for what purpose? For the purpose of being slaughtered for the harvest festival, that's what.

"Was man created just to work? If all you do is work and work, you are no better than the ox, which was made for work.

"Or do you suppose God made you just to bear children? Look at your neighbor's dog. It can have a litter of as many as eight puppies in one day. Is your purpose in life no better than a dog's?

"We were born, not as animals, but as human beings. The true purpose in life is to believe in Jesus, the Son of God, and to enter into the kingdom of God."

Jashil's mind raced back to the time she fell into the icy stream when she was seven, when she lost consciousness and would have died painlessly. At the exact moment of her fall a farmer carrying an empty A-frame on his back happened to come by. He rescued her even though he was known as the village idiot, retarded as he was. Had it been that God used him to snatch her from the jaws of death, from a rocky, icy stream? She wondered now.

The child in the tent was eager to be part of that greater reason for her life. But she was fascinated by a strange thing that happened right in front of her. A neighbor woman whose arm was twisted and deformed eased to the front. The preacher touched her and said something like, "In Jesus' name, your arm is restored." Jashil watched bug-eyed as the woman stretched out her arm and waved it in the air.

Jashil slipped out of the tent while the people were singing and clapping to the music and made her way to get Mama. Mama had migraine headaches; she just had to come to the tent right now and get well, like that neighbor with the twisted arm.

When she related the news at Mama's side, she staggered back dumbfounded to see Mama's reaction of anger. "Since when have you become a Jesus follower?" she demanded, then immediately went into a chant for purification: *"No moo-ah-mee-ta-pul.* Save us, merciful Buddha!"

While Mama kept that up for a few minutes, Jashil began to cry. She cried so much that Mama was moved. "Well, come on, come on," Mama said at last. "Let's go. Now dry those tears. Come on, let's go down there if it means that much to you."

"We have no right to claim the promises of God before we obey His commandments," the evangelist was saying as mother and daughter crawled under the tent. "Repent from loving false gods and trust Jesus Christ for what He claims to be, the very Son of God."

Mama listened, hearing for the first time some of the promises for a steady life. She waited her turn in a line of everybody who wanted to "expect something from God." After her brief moment with the preacher, she never had a migraine headache again, and Jashil thought her mother never ceased praying after attending that service. She prayed in Korean and she prayed in a language Jashil had never heard.

Life was different for the three of them. Jashil herself began to entertain hopes of an education. The wealthier kids in school teased her: "Ha, Jashil, we hear you're going to be a business woman. Too bad you don't have a father who can provide for you. When you get rich, buy us a meal in a restaurant!" They laughed and mocked. They seemed to always be saying, "My father this, my father that."

But Mama said, "Do you want to be a mere seamstress like your mother? If you do well in school, you can have a good job." Emphasizing every word, she deliberated slowly, "As long as you trust Jesus and study diligently, you will succeed." She made the order clear—trust Jesus first. It was written in the Bible that way too: "Seek ye first the kingdom of God, and his righteousness; and all these things shall be added unto you" (Matt. 6:33).

But it became harder and harder to put Christ first. Since 1930, the imperial government had pressed Shinto worship upon the churches and the Christian schools. (By persecuting the Christians, the Japanese authorities planned to increase the power of the Shinto spirits, according to Esther Ahn Kim, *If I Perish,* Moody Press: Chicago, 1977, p. 212). Both students and teachers were to bow before the state shrines, making their pilgrimage on the eighth day of every month as if circumcised into covenant with Japan, with Nationalism, commemorating the Pearl Harbor attack which had occurred on the eighth day of December, 1941. When the administration insisted that this was not a religious act but a patriotic one, some Methodists accepted the official reasoning; but the Presbyterians closed their schools instead of complying. Many pastors and laymen were imprisoned for "inordinate behavior," that is, their resistance to shrine worship. In the Bible, God had said, "Thou shalt have no other gods before me" (Exod. 20:3).

"Shinto" meant "way of the gods," or "god road," but Jesus had said, "I am the way, the truth, and the life: no man cometh unto the Father, but by me" (John 14:6).

The government required every household to purchase a Shinto ornament at the shrine, to hang it in their homes as a divine protectorate and to honor it. But the Bible had warned: "The graven images of their gods shall ye burn with fire: thou shalt not desire the silver or gold that is on them, nor take it unto thee, lest thou be snared therein: for it is an abomination to the Lord thy God. Neither shall thou bring an abomination into thine house, lest thou be a cursed thing like it: but thou shalt utterly detest it, and thou shalt utterly abhor it; for it is a cursed thing. All the commandments which I command thee this day shall ye observe to do, that you may live, and multiply, and go in and possess the land which the Lord sware unto your fathers" (Deut. 7:25, 26; 8:1).

The land of Korea was their own, and the only way to possess it was to obey God—even if it meant disobeying the Emperor. On the first of the month some of the students hid themselves in the restroom, others finding nooks wherever their bodies could squeeze into. They tried to stay in hiding to avoid the blasphemy of bowing to the shrines.

Jashil heard of the nurses' examination and told her mother she had decided to apply for it.

Out of 1,300 aspirants fifty applicants would be accepted for training. All were to be Japanese except for five. Five Koreans would be accepted for training.

"O God," she prayed, "you know all the suffering that has been my mother's lot in life. Give me courage and wisdom to succeed, in Jesus' name I ask you, so that I may be able to help her and Brother. Please, Jesus, help me to be like Esther of the Persian Empire in the Old Testament. Help me to contribute something to the women of my nation. Like my father, let me expend myself for the oppressed people of Korea, who are still under the iron grip of the Japanese."

When the test results were announced, she praised God. She made it, one of the five Koreans permitted to take the nurses' training. At age twenty, she finished the basic training in Pyongyang, and at twenty-one she was a full-fledged maternity nurse. In some circles of that day and locale, her duties were equivalent to those of an obstetrician, in others a midwife. As in any society lacking medical facilities, patients with broken arms were among the clientele, as well as patients with TB and other ailments great and small.

In order to receive three times the regular salary, she agreed to go to the dangerous border area along the Yalu River, where sometimes whole villages were murdered by Manchurian bandits. She had Jesus; she dared to stand against any odds.

Later she ran her own clinic in Pyongyang, soon becoming not only well known and busy but accumulating more than enough wealth to support the family. At that time she attended Second Presbyterian Church, where her mother became the head deaconess. Her mother frequently prayed throughout the night and wept before the Lord. There were times when Jashil opened the clinic even on Sunday; usually in Korea the Christians dropped everything to worship God together and thus show their allegiance on the first day of the week. They wanted the first of everything to go to Him, as if to prove their belief in the verse: "Seek ye first the kingdom of God. . ." (Matt. 6:33). But babies sometimes refused to wait until Monday to get born.

On April 29, 1940, Jashil Choi was married to Chang Ki Kim, a Navy man. She continued the clinic, though she herself then started having babies.

In her mother's eyes she became an adulteress, not because of any bad morals, but because of reversed priorities. Where she once put God first, she came to put money and success first. Her mother would read to her from the last book in the Bible: "Thou hast left thy first love. Remember therefore from whence thou art fallen, and repent. . ." (Rev. 2:4, 5).

By now over 200 churches were closed throughout Korea and 2,000 Christians in prison. Fifty church workers suffered martyrdom. About the time Sung Hae, who was later to become Yonggi Cho's wife, was born in 1942, the Japanese government stopped the use of denominational names among the churches. The Korean equivalent of the *Kyodan* among churches of Japan, the United Church of Christ, was formed by the Japanese government as an effort to exercise control, strictly enforcing the union on August 1, 1945. With their Pacific war efforts almost lost, Japan could not endure such hymns as "Onward, Christian Soldiers" or "Soldiers of Christ, Arise." What could these mean except that Christians were urging fellow adherents to form an army and attack the Japanese!

The imperial authorities prohibited the reading or exposition of the biblical books of Daniel and Revelation and any Scriptures dealing with the Second Coming of

Christ or eschatology, or the singing of hymns about that subject. Teachings on the Second Coming of Christ were prohibited by edict. It was treason to say a king was coming to rule the world. Japan was the ruler of one world, one household!

A pastor was arrested for preaching about the kingdom of heaven. A traitor in the eyes of the rulers, he was warned that there was only one kingdom here, and that was the kingdom of Japan.

The story of David and Goliath was forbidden when a government worker heard a Sunday school teacher pointing out that a weak man armed with righteousness was more powerful than a mighty enemy. To the Japanese, this was nothing but a direct instigation to the weak Koreans to fight the strong Japanese.

When the war ended and liberation came to Korea on Jashil's thirtieth birthday, August 15, 1945, the North came to be spelled with a capital "N," and in two weeks Soviet troops poured into the new "nation" down to the thirty-eighth parallel. Rumors spread that Korean government officials who had worked for the Japanese were to be rounded up and sent to Russia or Siberia along with anyone involved in independence movements. As Jashil's husband was in that category, he and her brother fled together to the American-patrolled southern half.

They sold some possessions and sewed or wrapped the money in wads of cloth tucked into the middle of large bundles of red peppers. In Namshi they were to disguise themselves as poor farmers who were on their way to Pyongyang and eventually slip into South Korea. "Refugee" in the Chinese characters literally meant "name dying" or one who leaves himself as if to die.

Meanwhile, the Communists came in with glowing promises, and Christians were released from prison. Others who had gone "underground" now came forward to rehabilitate the churches. In Pyongyang, one of the most serious problems concerned the Presbyterians who had yielded to the Japanese demand to worship at the shrine. Church workers requested a definite repentance from pastors and elders, bidding them to stay out of their pulpits for at least two months and then make public confession. During the two months, the deacons and church members conducted the services. Seminaries were also to be reestablished to train workers to fill the shoes of those who had died in prison.

Some questioned whether a "Judas" could be forgiven at all. Others cited Peter as one who had denied the Lord but was reinstated.

Immediately after the liberation, in the North there appeared organizations calling themselves Self-government Societies or National Establishment Preparatory Societies, the church taking a leading part in these movements. The Communists had reason for concern. The first political party organized in liberated Korea was the Christian Social Democratic Party. It was formed for the express purpose of standing for democracy and the reformation of society in line with Christian ideals. In each district, with the church as a center, a district branch became so strong that the Soviets grew nervous. One leader was beaten to death, others injured and the church building and homes of the executive committee badly damaged.

High-school students, most of them Christians, showed their anger in a demonstration against the Communists; and when 5,000 students gathered in Shin Wiju many students were shot.

In Pyongyang, a Christian Liberal Party was being organized by the Rev. Kim Hwa-Sik, but the day before the organizational meeting was to have taken place, Kim and forty others were arrested and either died in prison or disappeared.

March 1, 1946, was proposed as a celebration of the historic Three-One Declaration of Independence that had occurred nationwide twenty-seven years earlier, with the churches planning special memorial services. The Communists, however, counteracted by scheduling a People's Assembly for that day, to institute a government made by the people, the Communist government. The churches were forbidden to hold memorial services and were ordered to cooperate with the Communist plans.

In spite of arrests, the Christians went ahead with their plans. In Shin Wiju, the Communists led a mob into the church, wrecked the pulpit and dragged the pastor around the city on an ox cart, with insulting placards hung about his neck.

Following this, the Communists scheduled all-important affairs for Sunday, demanding that the Christians attend, and demanding that political lectures be given in the churches. The "election day" for Kim Il-Sung's puppet government was set for Sunday, November 3, 1946.

Churches were burned when their leaders failed to comply with the Communists' demands. Elders disappeared or their children were shot at school. "Liberation" from Japan had only thrown them to the lions.

Jashil made preparations to escape to the South, assuming that her husband and brother had made it to safety months ahead of her. With her mother and three small children, she left home in March of '46, and waited near the border until June, when she finally contacted a man experienced in helping runaways get to the South and who was willing to risk his life to take them across.

The guide owned an ox cart, as his legitimate business was hauling merchandise. His advice was to slip across on a rainy night. Seven days the Choi five waited and huddled together in cramped quarters, begging God for rain. Seven days after the preliminary arrangements it started to drizzle. All day the clouds teased but they did nothing more than wet the dirt. Jashil and her mother, and the children, all prayed for a downpour. At 10 o'clock that night the downpour came but not the peddler.

It was 1:00 A.M. before they left, Grandmother and the three children loaded inside the ox cart and covered completely. Jashil walked behind the cart, the guide walking ahead of the ox that pulled the load. A rainy night had been chosen, he explained, so that the Soviet patrol dogs could not pick up their scent.

The rain, the fog, the tide were all in their favor. "I don't mind the risk so much with people who have faith in God," the ox-driver said with some confidence. "This is the best fog I've ever had for such a night." Not one of the 200 sentry dogs barked this time. But it was a fearsome event when suddenly the Russian soldiers and their dogs started to move a few feet past them. Only moments earlier their guide had directed a halt and Jashil had aided her mother and the children out of the cart to lie prostrate on the ground and to press hands across the children's mouths in case of any utterance.

A sigh of relief went out from them the moment the driver announced, though in a whisper, "We have crossed into the South. But be quiet," he cautioned.

He kept on at a steady pace, and would not let them move just yet. Except for the slightest rhythm of the wheels it would have been a deafening silence. Until from behind them there sounded a piercing, "Stop! We command you to stop!"

The driver turned pale. "Oh, God! I didn't think they'd be out tonight!" Robbers! Knowing the North Koreans carried with them their life's savings to set up a new life in the free South, looters waited in ambush to pillage for personal gains.

Jashil prayed aloud, "O God, in Jesus' mighty name, I ask you for an idea, for a miracle to save us from this fate."

Her voice then immediately entered into an act as if planned for the stage: "Sir," she addressed the ox cart driver. "Sir, where is that gun you had when we started out?" In a bellowing voice, she seemed to get through to the driver.

Although having no gun, he picked up on his cue: "Oh, I have it all right. It's right here," he said in a brave voice.

"Okay, Son, it's time to get up! You've been sleeping long enough," she shouted to the covered cart. "We're approaching our destination. It's time for all you men to wake up!"

The robbers turned and ran the other way.

Her husband was now working at the Capitol in Seoul. Jashil continued making money on her own, first setting up a maternity clinic in the capital, then trying her hand in other ventures. She manufactured laundry soap, established a second clinic, started a match factory; she served on the churchwomen's evangelism committee and now was the mother of four.

When her son was one hundred days old, she gave a feast customary to Korean ways for Song Kwang. From ancient times when there was a high mortality rate among infants, Korean families were thankful and hopeful if a child made it to this hundred-day milestone.

In time she became a member of the Korean People's Independence Committee, one of three women on the committee, serving with Syngman Rhee, Ikhee Shin, and White Panther Kim.

Suddenly, right when South Korea seemed to be getting on her feet, a messenger came to Jashil's office with a warning to her. "You must flee from Seoul right now and hide somewhere in the country!

"They know all about your being the wife of a Naval officer and that you are a member of the Korean People's Independence Committee. They have come once to your house already to abduct you; for sure, they will come again. You have to leave now; you have no time to plan."

A tomato vendor was coming down the road, a large basket of tomatoes balanced on her head.

"Lady, I would like to buy all of your tomatoes."

"All of them?"

"Yes. And let's exchange dresses. I'll trade my new one

for your tattered one. And I would like to buy the basket also."

They changed clothes right there in the street. "Here. Here's extra money for you," Jashil said as she handed the farmer's wife an extra wad.

Looking like a village woman going to the market, she arrived home and got the children ready while packing a few belongings. They were on the move again.

Zigzagging their cart of rice and bean paste and tomatoes around the soldiers lying dead after the Communist attack, they made their way to the ferry pier. The first bridge had been bombed out already. On the ferry she wanted to be taken for a farmer's wife, so she continued her act. "Tomatoes anyone? Nice vine-ripened tomatoes here."

They took refuge in the Chongkye Mountains. Five years earlier they had retreated to the mountains near Shin Wiju. This time they were several months in hiding, she venturing each night to a cave to pray until dawn. Seoul was retaken on the twenty-eighth and the Communists left; 80 percent of downtown Seoul was in ruins.

Jashil moved the family to Chinhae to be with her husband. There she became owner and president of a spindle manufacturing company employing 150 workers. She was able to purchase a car and hire a private chauffeur. No more rickshaws for Jashil Choi.

Three things she left off now—church, family, and Bible. No more rickshaw and no more tithing. It had seemed easy to tithe a little from a little; but to tithe from thousands, it was not so easy.

Her mother nagged at her: "Labor not to be rich: cease

from thine own wisdom. Will thou set thine eyes upon that which is not? for riches certainly make themselves wings; they fly away as an eagle toward heaven" (Prov. 23:4, 5).

Also from James, chapter one: "Let the brother of low degree rejoice in that he is exalted: But the rich, in that he is made low: because as the flower of the grass he shall pass away. For the sun is no sooner risen with a burning heat, but it withereth the grass, and the flower thereof falleth, and the grace of the fashion of it perisheth: so also shall the rich man fade away in his ways" (James 1:9-11).

In a short while her mother grew sick, to the point of death. Her firstborn daughter also, sixteen-year-old Bokja, was struck by a car, and Jashil was running back and forth to care for one and then the other. "Jashil," her mother called to her one day, "dedicate your life to God and become a president of a company in the kingdom of God."

Adding something that sounded crazy, her mother never succeeded in shaking Jashil back to her senses: "When I die, bury me with Bokja. She's coming after me."

Bokja was sixteen. She was recovering nicely. What on earth could Mother have meant?

Her mother died. And ten days later, Bokja died.

Right after the funerals, the Korean currency was devalued and many investors lost their fortunes. Big businesses had bought from her on credit and now they could not pay.

The guilt over the death of her mother and then her daughter, the complete bankruptcy of her business—and by now the estrangement of her husband—drove her to an unbearable point. She could not face herself. She felt that since she had forsaken God, then He had also forsaken her. She decided to commit suicide.

Laying her plans carefully, she reasoned that if she fasted herself to death, this kind of suicide would be more acceptable to God. Leaving her three other children with relatives who had been sympathetic during the troubles, she made her way toward the mountains, stopping to have one last meal before she carried out her aims. A woman came up to her and called her by name: "Jashil, you are Jashil, aren't you?"

Her face looked familiar.

They had not met for twenty years. The woman, like Jashil, had come from North Korea.

"Jashil, listen, there is a revival going on. Won't you come with me tonight?"

No! She was adamant, refusing to be persuaded.

Yet, she wanted the friend to keep nudging her to go. A part of her wanted to be persuaded to attend the meeting. But for one whose plans of destruction are already laid, a certain balkiness exerts itself. Anyway, by Confucian ethics she preferred death as opposed to shame. It seemed that by dying one could restore his private virtue.

The former acquaintance from the North was either sensitive or stubborn, for she would not take no for an answer. Jashil went to the meeting.

About a thousand people were sitting on the ground clapping to the music and shouting, "Amen! Hallelujah!" How irreverent, she thought. Then the preacher stood up, an old man with white hair.

"Dear friends," he started, "have you ever wondered why you were created?" Jashil could not believe her ears.

She stopped up her ears with her fingers but heard anyway. "Were you created just to eat and drink? Hogs are regarded as the biggest eaters—"

Lee Song Bong! The very same preacher who had baptized her thirty years earlier. And now she was hearing the very same words that he had spoken to her needs back in North Korea.

"I confessed all my sins as the Holy Spirit brought them to my understanding and remembrance," she said later. "Three days of sins."

After praying with the evangelist again and deciding to give herself back to God, she asked him whether he could help her get into the Presbyterian Bible school. Surely there must be thousands of women all over Korea, she thought, on their way to destruction the same as she had been, and she felt compelled to help them. Hearing her pray after that, Rev. Lee carefully advised her that there was a fairly new Bible school in Seoul that might be willing to take her, the Full Gospel Bible Institute.

7

Frogs for Chicken

(1957-1965)

After Cho left home to attend Bible school, his mother quietly started going to church. She was always the family doer, Father the talker. One day when she came home from a service, she announced to Father that she had been baptized that day, not quite knowing how to prepare for his reaction.

"That's good, that's good," were the only words he said.

But when winter came and it was not so cold as it should have been, Father ranted and raved. "It's all because of the Christians in my family that I can't make a living," he raged. It was an unusual Korean winter, and too mild for Father's woolen underwear business. "We've got to have some snow or I won't be able to sell one pair of gloves!

"First my Eldest Son, now my wife. Why would they never listen to the voice of the sage, to Tao's wit? 'Let your wheels move only along old ruts, is the more excellent way.' "

Heaven and earth are ruthless; he agreed with all that

he had read.

Taoism teaches that "something and nothing produce each other; the difficult and the easy complement each other; the long and the short off-set each other; the high and the low incline towards each other; note and sound harmonize with each other; before and after follow each other."

Wasn't it true? Hence, snow and wool must produce a winter livelihood, he had figured it. Only thing, he could get the wool to produce the clothing, but what must he do to merit the snow?

He would make a trip to Seoul and have a talk with his wayward son. Lao Tzu had written, "A creature in its prime doing harm to the old is known as going against the way. That which goes against the way will come to an early end."

Anyway, as the oldest son he had responsibilities and Father set out to tell him so. If Father could not make a living for the family, then he would lay it on the shoulders of Eldest Son to provide for his brothers and sisters.

It was a long train ride from Pusan to Seoul and Father appeared unshaven and tired, but in time to be dragged off to chapel. In the testimony time the Bible school students all pledged to take some of Father's merchandise and try to sell it for him door-to-door and on the streets. Yonggi was the preacher's interpreter; but excited over seeing his father, he preached what he wanted his dad to hear, not always what the other speaker was saying. He prayed earnestly, "O God, bring salvation to my father. Bring salvation to my father."

Some of the sermon already made sense to Father. "A

man can receive nothing, except it be given him from heaven" (John 3:27). Snow had to come from heaven, that much he knew.

The other part was new to him. He might have heard it before, but had never listened. "He that believeth on him [Jesus] is not condemned, but he that believeth not is condemned already, because he hath not believed in the name of the only begotten Son of God. For God so loved the world, that he gave his only begotten Son, that whosoever believeth in him should not perish, but have everlasting life. For God sent not his Son into the world to condemn the world; but that the world through him might be saved" (John 3:18, 16, 17).

Here Father had come to get his own son to save him from the slump brought on by the mild winter, and his son stood telling him that Hananim's Son would be the one to save him. He knew about Hananim, but he never realized He had a Son. Here Yonggi was saying that Hananim's Son was the *way* (John 14:6). Tao had always told all about "the way." Indeed Taoism was called "the school of the way." But Tao had insisted the *way* is forever nameless, that the way that can be spoken of is not the constant way. Now Yonggi stood there saying clearly that Jesus is the way.

When the service was over and the chapel had cleared out, Eldest Son made his way to the back where Father sat with his head down, as if thinking. "Father, were you sleeping? Did you go to sleep during my sermon?" he chided.

Tears were falling down Father's face as he explained, "I could hardly look up there because of the man who stood in the middle behind you and the American."

"In the middle?"

"Yes, that man with blood on his forehead smiled at me and pointed his finger right at me. He was like a strange bright light and I could not keep looking; every time his light pointed to me, I could see all the shameful things I've ever done and even all the evil thoughts I've ever thought."

"Father, would you like to make all those things vanish and start all over like a baby's heart, pure and undefiled by all these years of your life up to now?"

Eldest Son led his father in a prayer of repentance, confessing his sins to God and receiving forgiveness. He had made the first step out of the old rut; he could walk a new way that led to life.

"Son, I have a question," he said. "Does the Bible invalidate all the wisdom I've ever learned from Tao and Confucius and Buddha? If Jesus is the way, then Tao is in error. But he seems so right in some of his other philosophies."

"Well, Father, the Bible says, 'There is a way that seemeth right unto a man, but the end thereof are the ways of death' " (Prov. 16:25).

The three great classics all had strong points of grave differences, Confucianism being politico-moral and ceremonial, Taoism rather religious and magical, and Buddhism dealing with metempsychosis and the future. Yet, Father had lumped them all together trying to follow them all, perhaps the same as countless other Asians—"just in case." While the Chinese founders of each of the three great religions had all lived in the sixth century before Christ, none of them had been deified until after his own death, and then by a society of man who searched desperately for a messiah to believe in.

How like man to rush things and do it his way, not waiting a little while longer for the revelation of God's way. Most of them ended up copying in some way the trinity idea, and the heavy use of the color red as the symbol of atoning blood but leaving out the Christ whose blood atoned; even the temples took on the form of the Jewish tabernacle with all its symbolic richness which God had explicitly directed Moses to build, later revealed as pictorial revelations of the characteristics of Christ and the Holy Spirit (Exod. 25:1-31:11; Heb. 8:1-10:22; Heb. 13:8-16).

Groping for a way out of the wilderness of life's problems, Buddhism took man out of the world as if to become a recluse in the mountains or in the woods if not in some costume strange to the times; Confucianism tried to build a society where man could face his problems, or at least pretend they did not exist. Christ, unlike the escapist way, came to interpret life, to broaden and deepen and sharpen man's awareness of life, to take him deeper into the real world, enable him not to run away but to understand his problems. While hedonism pursued pleasure as the means of temporarily forgetting the reality of problems, and the Stoics rejected pleasure and turned to serious reasoning as the only way, Christ offered joy plus understanding.

"I will put it this way, Father," Yonggi talked man-to-man with the Cho who sat across from him. "So much as I can understand so far, the philosophies do contain truth; man can live by them and society can profit from them— up to a point. But the Bible contains all truth, and only truth. The Bible also warns us that Satan himself is clothed as an angel of light in order to deceive us from the true and only way to God.

"So just be careful, Father. Follow God really and truly. God will direct you just as He promised. He is the perfect Father; from Him, you can get all the wisdom and knowledge you need to raise up those young children you have at home. If Tao has misled you on any part of the path, I know you will take care, for wise bees sip not from fallen flowers."

They talked a little further about the similarities and differences of this religion and that one. "The point is not to focus on their similarities but on the one central difference that makes the matter cut and dried," Yonggi exhorted. "In all the others there is one thing missing. If you make a building and you leave out the cornerstone, who would dare enter that building?

"Jesus Christ is the cornerstone. You look here in my Bible. Now read that: 'Jesus Christ . . . This is the stone which was set at nought of you builders, which is become the head of the corner. Neither is there salvation in any other: for there is none other name under heaven given among men, whereby we must be saved' " (Acts 4:10-12).

"That's it, Father," he said as they walked out of the chapel together. As they stepped outside they were surprised by the biting cold air. Snow! They jumped up and down as if they were two children.

"I can sell my gloves! I can sell my woolens! Oh, what a wonderful winter! We're going to make it, we're going to make it!" For the first time in years, father and son hugged and patted each other on the back and hugged again, forgetting themselves in the whiteness of the snow-covered ground and the silent flurry as of manna from heaven.

Over a hot bowl of noodles, Yonggi gave his father a Korean Bible and underlined Isaiah 1:18-20 to remember this day forever: "Come now, and let us reason together, saith the Lord: though your sins be as scarlet, they shall be as white as snow; though they be red like crimson, they shall be as wool. If ye be willing and obedient, ye shall eat the good of the land: But if ye refuse and rebel, ye shall be devoured with the sword: for the mouth of the Lord hath spoken it."

The mouth of the Lord had spoken, and tragedy came to Korea. By the tens and hundreds, Koreans died of the flu. The nation was hard hit, and Yonggi Cho was absent from classes. Unable to eat and burning with fever, he lay in the dorm, so sick that he had no hope to live.

The solemn news spread about the classrooms and the ping-pong table remained quiet. The chairman of the student body was dying.

In Korea there were thought to be ten things which were long-lived and deathless—man certainly not among them—the pine tree, the tortoise, rocks, the stag, clouds, the sun, the moon, the stork, water, and a certain moss which was called the ageless plant.

The administration summoned Jashil Choi and broke the school regulations to admit a female into the men's dorm. Being older than a regular student, and also a licensed nurse, she was told to go into his room and see what she could do for him.

As soon as she entered, she backed out of the room, shut the door and left. The room smelled of death. It was that unmistakable, odious omen that hovers over a body lying suspended between the living and the dead. She had smelled it too many times before. Walking briskly away, she stopped suddenly as if hearing a familiar voice call her name. "You are to pray for him. That man in the room is to be your son-in-law."

"What! That's impossible! If my daughter ever married that man, soon she would be a widow. He is a living corpse," she answered out loud before she realized there had been no audible voice. What she had known before as the voice of God, audible to her innermost being, had commanded her to pray for him.

She ran back to the room, flung open the door and went to his side. Even her hands burned as she touched his forehead and began to pray.

With his eyes cloudy and floating, he raised his eyelids and told her to wrap him in a straw mat and have him removed to a mountain. "Bury me anywhere," he instructed, "but don't tell my parents."

She gave him fruit and made him eat.

The next moment he vomited and seemed unable to catch hold of his breath again. "Oh, God, I've killed him. Please help him live. I'm sorry, God. In Jesus' name, help him live!"

Although he breathed, his face was gray and the fever would not subside. She thought he was dehydrating and had to have some liquid in his body. Bathing his hot forehead with a soothing rag, she prayed and thought, prayed and thought. She went to the store and made him a soup, praying the whole time.

"Eat it," she demanded. "You have to eat it." What illness was there for which soup was not the answer?

In obedience, he sipped one swallow.

"Eat more! Eat it all!"

Slowly, his energy too drained to hold the soup bowl, he swallowed it sip by sip, then turned and vomited it all upon the mat. His pulse beat wildly and his heart seemed to be having an attack. Jashil was frightened. But she was more frightened to see him calm down so suddenly and not open his eyes.

"Lord, have I killed him? Please, Jesus, do something quick! I won't force him to eat another bite."

She bathed his forehead, squeezing rags one after another, morning and night, for fifteen days.

"Hell is cooking my head," he spoke one day.

It was these days that united the work of their hands and hearts. "I'll call you mother," he told her after recovering from the grips of flu that year. "My mother gave me birth, and you gave me a second birth." There was a power in the touch of a human hand on a burning forehead, combined with the spoken prayer in Jesus' name. In sickness or in health, they prayed for each other. A bond had been formed, strange and wonderful.

Before graduation, one night in the worship service various people were praying and being prayed for. Cho felt prompted to stand beside Jashil Choi and pray especially for her. God gave him a prophetic word— that she would be divorced, and that in time her husband would come back to her. The prophecy also predicted that "this man who is praying for her now" would become her son-in-law.

Cho laughed at the third part. Why, her daughter was still a teen-age schoolgirl in pigtails.

Following winter graduation in March, 1958, Cho was preparing to further his studies in America. However, feeling a strong tie, if not a definite responsibility, to Pastor Choi, after all she had done for him, he agreed to work with her for a short time to help get her church going in the Taejo Dong area of Seoul.

"Won't you build even a small brick house before the rainy season for your children, Minister Choi?" he urged her. "What are you going to do?" By now, she was divorced with three children to care for and her debtors still owed her money.

"Well, don't worry about that. Building a house is not the most important thing for me now. Instead, Pastor Cho, won't you work with me to gather thirty persons as my church members before you go to America? Anyway, I have to buy bricks and cement and I have no money right now. I have to wait and collect from those who still owe me."

"No, never mind. Let's start, not with money, but with faith," the youthful Cho insisted.

"No, no, you never do that way without any plan, Pastor Cho. We can't do so now."

As always, she acted as the balancing power. His first year in Bible school, when he had been disgusted with the easy curriculum and wanted to quit, she had encouraged him to stay. Now she was urging a practical way for the building program, to build the congregation first and then the mortar.

He preferred the proverbial way: If you want to catch fish, first build a net.

They managed to buy a tent from the U.S. Army and by

sewing and patching it frequently, they were able to use it and they placed straw mats over the bare ground to sit on. The Han River banks were still crowded with shacks in 1958, only five years since the aftermath of the Communist war. The Assemblies of God mission had started in Korea by giving out relief and establishing orphanages. The church would initially come from those of similar need, people who had no desire to sit around and philosophize but rather who were hungry or crippled, people who had been broken in spirit as well as body.

Choi determined that she did not need a house; Cho determined that she did. He went out and came back with a carpenter. They built a house. Shortly afterward, Typhoon Sarah brought down the tent, beyond repair. The house had been done in good timing.

Jashil Choi visited house to house and Cho took charge of what to say to them whenever they came to church. Before one or five, he preached as if seeing thirty seated before him. He stressed what he called the here-and-now of the gospel, plus love. He had heard ministers who talked only about heaven, but Cho had just come out of a two-year course of study where he felt that ministers were trained to make a living by their mouths and he did not like it. Idealistic, youthful, and angry, he preached the gospel for the present life. "In social ways it was absolutely impossible for me to help my society," he confessed later, "so I had to help the people rehabilitate their thinking, to help their present life."

Ultimate rehabilitation does not come from outside, he reiterated. Thus complementing the social relief program of the various missions organizations, his messages endeavored to challenge defeated beings to live victorious lives. For the first twelve years of his ministry, Cho's message centered around three points: "hereness," "nowness," and love.

TB patients demoniacs, the depressed, thieves, and children ventured to attend church services. Some of the ill were sick enough to spit up blood and phlegm, a scene all too familiar to the lanky twenty-two-year-old who did the preaching.

Mother Choi boiled plenty of corn to feed them all. They could take in about thirty persons in the inner room, the opposite room, and the main floor in the house.

When her oldest son contracted acute pneumonia, she prayed throughout the night. In her house visits she had told the neighbors that God heals. If we believe God to heal the people who come to the meetings, how can we put my son in the hospital, she reasoned. Praising God in spite of the predicament, she determined to set up her son as a model case.

She separated him from the other sick people and gave him a special diet, praying the whole time. "Oh, Lord, as Abraham presented his son to you, so I do now present my son. Please show us your glory by this boy. In the name of Jesus, I do ask. Amen."

Ten days later the boy was completely well.

Because of this example in the neighborhood, more and more people came to church. Unable to hold them all in the house, they pitched a second tent in front of the Choi house. Soon it was stitched in so many places they could hardly find another place to sew it again; but it held up.

Children always ran to the tent whenever it rained.

"What are those tin cans for?" Cho asked them.

"When it rains the frogs come."

"Naughty children. Whenever I ask you to come to church on Sunday, you don't come; but you come to the tent to catch frogs. Why do you catch frogs?"

"We boil them for chicken."

Cho laughed and thought God was helping the church to also supply relief to the needy—in the form of frogs for children.

On Sunday morning Cho would go up to the hill and cry out in a loud voice, "It's time for church! Come to church!" Having no watch, he nevertheless became the neighborhood chimes, though some called him the cuckoo. He imagined himself to be a shepherd calling to the sheep. They eventually hung an iron pipe large enough in diameter to sound somewhat like a bell when they struck it.

Still Yonggi had no desk or paper on which to prepare his sermons. He picked up pencil stubs wherever he could find them and fashioned a slender bamboo stick as the holder to make the pencils long enough for writing. Picking discarded newspapers out of the city trash, he wrote sermon outlines around the margins. If the first words fail, ten thousand would not avail, he thought; hence his sermons were to the point with no marginal waste.

Not by choice but of necessity they lived in the same poverty as the people they served. Fasting was a frequent practice of Korean pastors after the war, as food was not always available. Anyway, they always said a full teapot made no sound.

One family whom Cho and Mother Choi visited had ten children but was one of the worst homes they had ever seen.

seen. They had nothing, yet the husband was an alcoholic. He had once been addicted to narcotics. His nephew, the president of a leading medical college in Korea, tried every means to cure his uncle of drug addiction but when everything failed, the nephew advised him to switch from drugs to alcohol. By now the man drank from early morning until late at night. His young boys tried to make some money shining shoes, but any money they made, their father took from them in order to buy whiskey. His penniless wife and children lived like beggars.

When the pastor had a talk with her about believing in Jesus, she was skinny and depressed because of heart trouble and stomach pains. Not wanting to hear, she said, "I just want to die. Life is like a machine—it has to have fuel, which passes through the body and is then eliminated. That's all. And someday it quits and doesn't run any more; that's the end. I just want to hurry up and finish life. That's the best thing that could happen. But I have a family, so I will not commit suicide. Won't you kill me? Please kill me. If you actually want to help me, kill me. Kill me!"

"I didn't come here to kill you. I came here to bring you life."

"I don't care about heaven; I'm not worried about hell. I've already been living in hell a long time."

"Sister, would you like to see your life changed? Would you like to see your husband changed? Would you like to see Jesus Christ come into your house and make your home beautiful?"

"Impossible, preacher; impossible! You're full of words. Only two kinds of men are any good—the buried and the unborn. You don't live in this mess. You don't know what it's like."

"Jesus Christ came to give you His grace. He himself lived in a stable. Grace is His gift to you, which you don't have to earn. He promised that His grace is sufficient to meet every need. Christianity is not just a religion. It's more than ethics or good teachings. Jesus Christ comes and gives you His grace and makes you beautiful."

Not even knowing why she came, the woman started visiting the church whenever she heard the gong from the hill. She was surprised when she stopped having stomach pains and heart trouble; her depression turned into a smile and her personality changed, perhaps to what it had been before she got married. She went about humming a tune and her children's behavior improved in spite of their home conditions.

Together she started praying with the pastor for her husband. "It's going to take more than prayers to change that man," the neighbors laughed. At times he himself came to the church to ridicule them.

"If heaven made him, earth can find some use for him," they quoted from the Chinese proverbs familiar to them all and persisted in prayer, asking Jesus to deliver him from his condition.

Constantly interrupted by his drunken threats and vociferous derisions, the small congregation was tested and exasperated. Could they change a leopard's spots? Some of the housewives expressed their doubts; the wife feeling sorry that her husband kept causing trouble, offered to stay away from the group. "One rat dropping spoils a pot of rice," she lamented.

But they were urged to keep on praying. If they were

praying, they wouldn't be discouraging each other so much. Like other Koreans, some in the neighborhood got up at four o'clock to pray together. One morning after Cho had awakened for early morning prayer meeting he felt as if he were falling into a deep sleep, then suddenly he felt his spirit was lifted and he saw the glory of heaven. Clearly he heard the words, "My son, I have heard your prayers."

He jumped from his bed, dressed and ran to his co-worker. "Mother, Jesus has heard our prayers!"

But one of the sons of the alcoholic came running into the house with a note in his hand. "Come quickly. He is dying."

When the pastors arrived, his wife explained how he had locked them inside and threatened to kill the family all through the night. But Cho, feeling sure he had heard the Lord's voice assure him that all was going to be all right, rebuked Satan as if he was speaking to a visible enemy in the room. Discerning that the man's screaming and dying act were caused by the oppressive spirit of the devil, they talked to the spirit of oppression as one might talk to someone in an adjoining room of the house.

Jesus' death on the cross was for present victory, they said, and man was simply to claim it as his rightful inheritance. The raging man instantly fell into a deep sleep. It had seemed like the time the disciples at sea were in danger of the raging storm and Jesus arose and rebuked the wind and the raging of the water, and they ceased and there was a calm (Luke 8:22-25).

The man continued sleeping quietly, and in those moments Jesus changed him; he never touched alcohol again, for its taste was repulsive to him. His personality began to change and he became gentle with each of his children and with his wife.

Neighbors started helping him and one friend bought a small bag of rice and gave it to him. He had not brought rice home in ten years; his wife was so moved that she began to cry. The same day she took out one-tenth of the rice to give as her tithe to the church; but she poured it back. "God, you know we need this rice; you will understand if we don't give tithes on this." Three times she took it out and three times poured it back. Her inner struggle was intense. But when she came to the 4:00 A.M. prayer meeting she came running, bringing one-tenth of the rice. She was crying so hard that she could hardly see the road, spilling the rice as she ran. Cho wanted to hand the rice back to her because he knew they had more children to feed than the Choi family had, and even the church group managed to have enough whenever they all ate together. But in her heart she was giving to God, not to them; he stood only as a symbol, as the servant of the Lord. So he prayed for her and blessed her in the name of Jesus: "It is more blessed to give than to receive" (Acts 20:35).

After two months had passed she was talking among the women. "We have been eating from this sack of rice for two months, all twelve of us, morning and night. This morning my husband asked me how I was managing because he had brought only one small sack of rice; but it's still lasting!" The pastors visited the house and looked at the mysterious rice. There was exactly one-tenth, the amount her tithe had been, remaining in the bottom of the sack. Every time she took out some rice and boiled it to eat there was always one-tenth remaining. Until her husband got a job and brought home another sack of rice, they could never consume it below that level no matter how regularly they dipped into it. When he brought in the next sack, the first one soon became empty.

"Give, and it will be given to you" was a biblical principle. "Good measure, pressed down, and shaken together, running over, they will pour into your lap. For whatever measures you deal out to others, it will be dealt to you in return" (Luke 6:38 NAS).

Yonggi Cho used to say he was going to America to study whenever the church grew to thirty members. But they started having all-night prayer and singing in the tent, and even when there were fifty members he did not leave.

To his themes "here, now, and love," there was added a fourth element of truth which he came to understand through experience—that is, specific prayer. It took awhile before he started putting this principle into practice, but it became one of several turning points in his life and ministry.

Boldly he prayed, asking God for improved living conditions. Looking about his bare room containing only the mat that he slept on, he started praying for three things— a table where he could eat and study, a chair, and a bicycle. He read in the Bible that "ye have not, because ye ask not" (James 4:2). He knew this meant asking God rather than man.

"Therefore, I say unto you, What things soever ye desire, when ye pray, believe that ye receive them, and ye shall have them" (Mark 11:24).

"Ask and it shall be given you" (Matt. 7:7).

Ask, ask, ask. The Bible was full of promises, *if a person asked.*

"All things, whatsoever ye shall ask in prayer, believing, ye shall receive" (Matt. 21:22).

"And whatsoever we ask, we receive of him, because we keep his commandments, and do those things that are pleasing in his sight" (1 John 3:22).

"And whatsoever ye shall ask in my name, that will I do, that the Father may be glorified in the Son. If ye shall ask any thing in my name, I will do it" (John 14:13-14).

"Ye have not chosen me, but I have chosen you, and ordained you, that ye should go and bring forth fruit, and that your fruit should remain: that whatsoever ye shall ask of the Father in my name, he may give it you" (John 15:16).

It was Jesus who had spoken all those things. Did He really mean "anything," or "whatsoever"?

Yonggi did not beg. But he asked. And he asked humbly. "Not because I deserve them, Father, but because you have given a purpose to my life and you have given me a job to do, to help people know the truth and be saved. Because you are the good Father who desires to give His children good gifts, I ask you please for a humble table, a chair, and a bicycle. In Jesus' name. Amen."

Just as the telephone downtown was an extension of someone's voice, and the pencil an extension of one's own thoughts flowing down the fingers, so the bicycle would extend his feet. He could visit more homes and make better progress with the time in one day, if only he had a bicycle.

He tried to muster up faith to believe he could receive

whatsoever he asked. Two months passed, three months, half a year.

"Well God, what's happened? Why can't I receive those things I asked for?"

What kind of chair do you want?

Huh? Clearly in his mind he had been pricked with a question.

"Father, is that you?"

I heard your prayer six months ago. But you must say clearly what kind of chair, table and bicycle you are requesting.

Maybe he made it up, but the urging was from a real source. He had not considered it before. So he acted on the impulse, on the "voice," whatever it was. It seemed to demand a response. It was as if an order from a department store was too vague and required which color and style the customer wished to have delivered.

It was a fascinating concept, that God would take time bothering to please him on something no doubt so mundane as two pieces of furniture and a bicycle. He thought for a moment.

"Well, Lord, I'd like to have a strong table, one that does not wobble around whenever I rest my elbows on it and try to write; a table made out of Philippine mahogany, please, with strong iron legs.

"And let's see, about the chair—honestly, Father, I would like one of those chairs that rolls around and I can swivel about in.

"Now, as for the bicycle, I would prefer a bicycle made in the U.S.A. The bicycles made in Japan right now are flimsy. Please give me a strong one from America."

This time he felt his faith surge with new hope. At church he announced he had a bicycle, a chair and a table. He felt good.

But following the service, two of the men asked whether they might see his new improvements. This, he had not anticipated. "Well, faith is like your two arms hanging down beside your body." He talked for talk's sake, stalling for time, hoping the men would not pursue their plan of going home with him to see his bicycle, table and chair. "You don't necessarily have to feel your arms hanging there in order to believe they are there, do you? Faith is the same way—if you believe in God, then you have faith, whether you can feel it or not. But like your hand, you have to use it before it can do you any good. Unused faith will wither like unused arms."

The men went home with him to his room and sat on the straw mat on the dirt floor. "Pastor, where are your chair, table and bicycle? Have you lied to us? You told us you had them."

He prayed earnestly for a way to answer, his face distraught and his lips silent. When he opened his mouth at last, his own words surprised him. "Sir, before you were born, did you exist?"

"Of course I existed. What does that have to do with this?"

"Where were you?"

"In Mama, of course."

"Could Mama see you?"

"No, but I was there."

"Exactly!" Patting his stomach with his hands, Cho made the parallel complete: "My bicycle, chair and table are in me. I know they are in me; and when the time is ready you will see them."

As if they had heard the joke of the year, both men tumbled out of the pastor's room, laughing and joking their way back up the road. For the next few weeks the housewives at the market laughed when they saw him. "Poor young pastor," they would shake their heads in pity. Some of the more forward type ran to greet him in the road and gesture, "My, how big you are getting! When are you due for delivery, sir?"

No one was able to forget the pastor's "pregnancy," so he developed a sermon on "pregnant prayer" to have ready whenever the triplets arrived.

Meanwhile the work went on. A messenger came to ask whether he could take time to help an American family who were packing to return to the United States. Eager for the chance to use English again and to be away from his environment for a day or two, he accepted the part-time work and hurried to the designated location.

Starting in the garage, he could hardly stand it when the American woman pointed to a bicycle in the corner and asked whether he knew where they might sell it. Made in U.S.A.! "Father!" Cho prayed silently, "Father. That's my bicycle! Thank you for showing me my bicycle. Don't let them sell it, Father. That's my bicycle!"

Upstairs he was packing books and files and office-type things when the woman of the house came and said to him, "I don't suppose you could use a table and chair, could you? We can't ship everything, and that desk and this chair we're going to have to leave here."

His heart pounded! Iron legs. Philippine mahogany.

And in the chair he pivoted to his heart's content.

"And, by the way, whatever is inside the desk drawer, if you can use it, take that too. Okay?"

Some pencils that had just been sharpened. An eraser. A ruler. Some paper clips. And a whole stack of white paper. He could not hold back the tears. A whole stack of white paper.

The Bible proved right again: "Eye hath not seen, nor ear heard, neither have entered into the heart of man, the things which God has prepared for them that love him" (1 Cor. 2:9).

Cho had a new sermon, in the words of Paul, "For this cause I bow my knees unto the Father of our Lord Jesus Christ, Of whom the whole family in heaven and earth is named, That he would grant you according to the riches of his glory, to be strengthened with might by his Spirit in the inner man; That Christ may dwell in your hearts by faith; that ye, being rooted and grounded in love, May be able to comprehend with all saints what is the breadth, and length, and depth, and height; And to know the love of Christ, which passeth knowledge, that ye might be filled with all the fulness of God. Now unto him that is able to do exceeding abundantly above all that we ask or think, according to the power that worketh in us, Unto him be glory in the church by Christ Jesus throughout all ages, world without end. Amen" (Eph. 3:14-21).

As the packing went on, the man and woman had a quick consultation upstairs and decided to "give the bicycle to the Korean boy." When the day was finished, Cho carried the bicycle home on his back. He had not asked nor said a word to the Americans about his hopes, but he had asked

Jesus to keep them from selling it. He did the best job of packing he had ever done in his life, his gratitude overflowing.

The church also started to really believe.

During his third year of church work, the government drafted Cho into the R.O.K. Army. Prior to the draft call, his pastoral license had been revoked by the Assemblies of God mission. It was one problem on top of another. Yonggi Cho was growing too big too fast, for one thing; age is respected in Korea, and one dare not become too successful, too early. For a swift arrow, he had pulled hard on the string, they might say. Another issue was over what the Bible called "other languages" or "tongues." His mission at that time advised him that they did not conduct their meetings as he was doing, and that he should study the Scriptures more carefully in light of modern theology.

A new missionary, Rev. John Hurston, was back in Korea, however, and he seemed to believe in Cho. He wanted to help the young fledgling. Cho had served as an able interpreter when Hurston spoke on an evangelistic tour in Korea in 1958, having come from the United States after mission service in Africa.

Women were not ordained in the Korean mission and anyway Jashil Choi felt strongly that her place was not behind the pulpit but on her knees. Prayer and fasting, she could do, but she believed the main speaker and pastor should be a man. By knocking on doors and helping the sick, she would serve every waking moment. For the duration of Cho's stint in the Army, John Hurston came to work with her and the church.

During a revival meeting which they conducted at Pul

Kwon Dong, 200 new members were added to the church. "We don't know what happened," explained Hurston. "We went to bed one night and woke up with a church."

On October 15, 1961, they moved to the Sodaemoon West Gate area downtown, calling themselves the Revival Center. Starting with a tent and later advancing to a pre-fabricated structure shipped from the United States, the accommodations served the more than 500-member congregation and seemed to add new life to post-war Korea, as the name suggested.

"Pray for Pastor Cho's discharge from the Army!" urged Mrs. Choi.

"Oh, when I first started praying for that, I had a revelation from the Lord that he would be in the Army only seven months," related Hurston, not understanding why. Hurston never asked again; he sometimes thanked the Lord for Cho's release and went on expecting to see him at the end of seven months.

Yonggi Cho, in the special division of Army Intelligence, developed stomach disorders and underwent an emergency operation that lasted eight hours. When this ordeal was over, he received a medical discharge and returned to help lead the church then located at West Gate. He had been in the Army seven months.

Not only the women of the church, but also Cho and Hurston, went to homes, visited the sick, and invited the down-and-out to experience a new way of life. They held early morning prayer meetings, Hurston constantly driving home the same point: "Not by might, nor by power, but by my spirit, saith the Lord of hosts" (Zech. 4:6).

"The Holy Spirit has got to build the church, Pastor Cho.

Man can't do it." Over and over, Hurston seemed to have one theme. "Except the Lord build the house, they labor in vain that build it" (Ps. 127:1).

On the day of the dedication of the new building, February 18, 1962, a crippled man crawled in on his knees. He left the services walking normally. A man in his sixties had lost his hearing in both ears; he came to be healed and he was, his hearing completely restored.

Church growth shot upward. The aim was not church growth, but ministry of the life of Christ. The church was there "to preach the gospel to the poor; . . . to heal the brokenhearted, to preach deliverance to the captives, and recovering of sight to the blind, to set at liberty them that are bruised, To preach the acceptable year of the Lord" (Luke 4:18-19). And so the church grew.

On May 13, 1962, the name of the Revival Center was changed to Full Gospel Central Church. The Koreans had a saying that a buried fire will flare up; out of the ashes of the nation the church had revived. Now it was time to concentrate on building a strong and stable congregation, centralizing on the full gospel and not revival only. Whenever God changed someone in the Scriptures He changed the person's name first. Before giving Abram a son, He changed his name to "Abraham," meaning "the father of many nations." Jacob, "the supplanter," was changed to Israel, "the prince." Simon, "the reed," was changed to Peter, "the small rock." "Saul" of Tarsus, who had persecuted the Christians of his day, was changed from the man he had tried to be in his own winsome way to be made "Paul," meaning "little."

The church in Seoul required a name change in order to

function as the church.

Cho's ministerial license was reinstated after a couple of years and Hurston stepped down to the position of associate pastor, elevating Cho to the leadership position. It had not really mattered. "I couldn't really speak the language," said Hurston. "What good is a pastor of the people if he can't speak with them heart to heart on an everyday level? Cho had been serving as their pastor all along; I was merely holding the position for him until he got the paper back that made it legal for him to be there."

Missions and missionaries in those days were the scaffold used in constructing a lasting work inside, and when the construction was finished, the scaffolding was disassembled and moved on, letting the newly finished piece of work function on its own. Nevertheless, Cho had in fact resented Hurston for any success in church growth and feared the missionary was trying to take the church away from him. He now worked harder than ever, as if in competition with the world.

Then in 1964, he had a nervous breakdown. The West Gate facilities were enlarged with a 500-seat balcony, but the membership of two thousand necessitated holding four services on Sunday. In one service, after baptizing others for two hours and interpreting for a guest speaker, Cho fainted while preaching and was taken to a hospital.

Doctors advised him to change professions.

Change professions? "I'm a minister. I can't change my profession," he argued.

The doctor suggested he go into business or do something he could work at from eight to five, leaving his mind free from such round-the-clock involvement. He rested in the hospital, the doctors refusing to release him all week. The next Sunday he persuaded some deacons to come and take him to the church so that he could preach again. Holding onto the pulpit, he preached for eight minutes and then fell. He was taken back to the hospital, determined to conquer his health dilemma.

For relaxation he started to read the Bible through, beginning from page one, but he got stuck in Exodus. He was especially startled by the words to Moses: "You will surely wear out, both yourself and these people who are with you, for the task is too heavy for you; you cannot do it alone" (Exod. 18:18 NAS).

It was not exactly clear to him, but something in the advice of Moses' father-in-law, Jethro, seemed to offer the key to the present problem and the future life of the church. You shall place leaders of thousands, of hundreds, of fifties and of tens, Jethro had counseled, and Moses obeyed.

Cho reasoned with the doctors that he had read a workable solution in the Old Testament and that he was able to leave the hospital without risking a relapse; and the doctors reasoned with Cho that he would take a long time to fully recover, needing plenty of fresh air and recreation. Both proved right. In fact, it took almost five years to gain back what he had lost. His concentration span was shortened, his memory often failed him, he grew tired easily, and he had sleepless nights without reason. He was forced to swim and golf, to take walks and hikes; what to him was a loss of time turned out to be the medications necessary to his health, both mental and physical.

At twenty-eight, he had tried to do everything himself,

to monopolize the church; as the church grew, so did the responsibilities. Like Moses, he had tried to solve every situation. Cho performed all the weddings, all the baptisms, preached all the funerals, planned the services, prayed for the sick. In his own eyes he had become the mighty Cho. Now Jethro was telling him to select able men out of all the people. It had been easier to bend his body than his mind. Now he must learn to live within the limits of the responsibility which fell to him.

In obedience to the Bible as well as to his failing body, he called for the church deacons and deaconesses. "From now on you will be the ones to pray for the sick, to plan the services, and to reach out your hand in the name of Jesus in whatever He shows you to do. You are ministers of God."

"But, Pastor, we've not been trained."

"Well, you go back and read the New Testament and then come and tell me whether you think you have to have seminary training before you can minister to the people. I will train you, and you will go and carry out the roles of the church."

"Pastor, we've never been given such responsibilities, we've never been trusted." Some wept. "We're not worthy. We're not good enough. There are others better than we are."

He held up ten fingers. "Even your own ten fingers are unequal," he showed them. They were not being commissioned because they were good. He was not a preacher because he was good.

At first they were reluctant and inhibited. In time, however, they began to function as the leaders they had been called to be.

By now the man who had been an alcoholic and mistreated his family had been coming to church regularly, had been baptized and was sending his children to school. Their home had become a beautiful place, alive and happy. When he was made an elder and instructed to lead ten and then fifty, he became a dynamic leader according to the Jethro plan. In Korea there was an age-old saying, "What do fine horsemen know of aching feet?" His own way had been rocky, so to speak; and having known the miseries of a godless life, he really led them as one who had walked the road and who knew the path to a better life. He was compassionate; he was strong. Two of his children later became ministers.

As the church continued to increase, Cho began to feel dismantled. Did the church even need him any more? He was utterly broken. Somewhere there lay a fine balance between designating authority and retaining one's self-worth; truly all men had the need to be needed. Cho desperately needed to find that balance.

The following year Cho entered what he privately called "the new March First agreement"—on March 1, 1965, he married Sung Hae Kim, the daughter of Jashil Choi. (In Korea it is customary for women to retain their father's surname throughout life, hence Jashil has always used the name Choi, though her children are surnamed Kim in honor of their father.) Cho was twenty-nine; Sung Hae would be twenty-three on June 10. Sung Hae was an accomplished musician and graduate of the prestigious Ewha Women's University, the largest Christian women's university in the world. At the wedding, the groom almost fainted as he had done at his grandfather's funeral a decade before. Was his courage so anemic? He loved his bride's mother as his own family; for nine years they had been through thick and thin together. But from today he was being implored to love her daughter as his own body, to love her just as Christ did the church.

"Husbands, love your wives, even as Christ also loved the church, and gave himself for it. . . . So ought men to love their wives as their own bodies. He that loveth his wife loveth himself. . . . For this cause shall a man leave his father and mother, and shall be joined unto his wife, and they two shall be one flesh. This is a great mystery: but I speak concerning Christ and the church. Nevertheless let every one of you in particular so love his wife even as himself; and the wife see that she reverence her husband" (Eph. 5:25-33).

In younger days when the church was beginning at the tent site they had sat at the same table; he felt more like a big brother in the same family. He loved the church. Now he wondered whether he could really love a wife.

8

Speak Out

(1966-1978)

"You heal all those people who come to the church lame and deaf. Why can't you heal our own baby?" his wife stormed out at him.

"I don't heal. It's Jesus who heals!" he lashed back at her.

Their infant son's attacks of asthma had kept them awake again. Torn between their own need of sleep and their sympathy for the boy in the crib, the husband and wife seemed constantly at war. They argued over God, they argued over the doctors, they argued over whose turn it was to get some rest while the other one looked after Hee Jae. They argued over whose fault it was that they had had so much trouble with the baby in the first place.

Born the first year of the marriage, he was a hindrance to all his pastor-father wanted to see accomplished. He was a drain on his mother's frail condition. Having had TB in high school, she had been extremely weak during the pregnancy and her doctor had advised an abortion. Unable to reconcile such an action with his position in the church, Cho had risked the birth instead; now his wife's body needed rest. At the same time, he needed to recover from his own condition. The nervous breakdown he had suffered only a year before left him tense; hypertension and stress ruled their lives and commanded their home.

Laying his hand on the baby for what seemed like the millionth time, as if laying clay on clay, Cho cried out to Jesus Christ, "Hear me, Lord. Please hear me this time, Lord. . . ."

After asking as clearly as he knew how for a miracle, he sat alone with his head between his hands, and tried to understand what was happening. The previous Sunday a young woman had come to the platform at the worship service; she had been unable to hear a word since birth, and now she came with her cousin to be healed. Cho had been uneasy. What if he declared her healed in the name of Jesus in front of all those people and nothing happened? He had put his finger to the girl's ear and prayed more than once before daring to take his hand away and claim the results.

After this prayer, he slowly removed his finger and stepped behind the girl on the stage. He clapped his hands and she flinched. "Mother," he whispered.

"Mother," she repeated. She had heard!

Softly he spoke behind her ear again, "Hallelujah!"

And she repeated, "Hallelujah!"

Doctors checked case after case of reported miracle healings and did so again months later to verify the fact. By now various medical doctors had made this their church and occasionally would bring a patient to the pastor's office for prayer.

But why must his own child lie helplessly struggling for

his next breath? He had called for the elders of the church to anoint the child with oil and pray the prayer of faith; they had confessed faults to one another, as James had written (James 5:14-16). Still nothing happened.

Asthma was a stopped-up condition from which the baby could hardly get release. And yet the child harbored no grudges nor unforgiveness, no hatred nor resentments and jealousy—the things that stopped so many from enjoying free health.

The young father sat and sat, reading, praying, thinking, worrying. This was his own flesh of his flesh, blood of his blood. As Jesus was to the Father, so Hee Jae became to Yonggi Cho. He loved the boy in the crib, tiny though he was. How his own father and mother in Pusan must also love him, their own son. The Chinese saying became so true to him in these moments: "To understand your parents' love, bear your own children."

"God, please God, release Hee Jae from this awful asthma. In the name of Jesus, whom you love with your whole heart. And Lord, forgive me for resenting him for intruding on my ambitions."

The crib was quiet. Frightfully quiet. Cho dashed to the side of it and shook the baby. The wheezy breathing had stopped and the room seemed muffled in silence. He was sleeping. For the first time, he was sleeping restfully, his mouth was closed and he was breathing quietly through his nose; his chest rose and fell rhythmically. Could it be that he was going to be all right?

Sung Hae woke up from a nap and hastened to the baby's side. She touched him to be sure; he seemed to be breathing, and he felt warm and soft. "What happened?" She looked at the man sitting in the chair.

"I don't know," was all he answered.

The room was still. "Jesus must have healed him, is all I know," he said softly.

He could not tell why his little son had been made well, nor why he had come into the world sick. He did not understand why an innocent baby had had to suffer long nights of agony and misery, why God had not healed him in the services at church or through the hands of the elders.

In the pastor's mind were a lot of questions for which he had no answers. "When I die and go to heaven someday I'll ask the Lord why some are healed and others are not," he said quietly to his wife, whose name in English would mean "holy grace."

Cho went out to take a walk. He had watched the trees turn yellow, brown, and then become bare. He imagined it was spring when the swallows would slice through the air again. His son would one day run about and grow, even as new leaves promised to bud tender green to feed the eyes with hope. Always he had believed faith was stronger than so-called reality. Yet God had healed his son when he himself was void of faith. Out of divine mercy God performed a miracle no man deserved; could it be that sickness, too, was not deserved? Did the trees deserve to be bare? Must nature have faith for green to appear? God and His merciful kindness were not to be fully understood, but this father who walked the streets in Seoul was thankful his son had breathed. "I give him to you, Father, just as you have given him twice to me. I don't know how to raise a child, but I'll do my best for you. Teach my wife how to raise him, and strengthen her body and give her health, I pray."

A person always makes progress, Cho thought, every day learning something he did not know the day before. Hesse had said that even so, you never reach a great height from which you suddenly see new vistas.[22] Here is where he thought he must part with the author of that philosophy. Hadn't God shown Moses a panoramic view of Canaan and the elevated life He had planned for the people? Hadn't God shown Paul a continent beyond the Jewish world, a Gentile phenomenon that even Peter and John in all their boldness had not seen before?

Why, even though he was an unknown preacher in Korea, God had shown him new vistas all along. God had taught him how to pray specifically rather than in general, rambling words. God had taught him to be venturesome, to dare to claim the crippled would walk and the deaf would hear. God had shown him to name a thing into success, including church leaders by calling them leaders. God had taught him to dream. When he had preached to a congregation of five, he had imagined preaching to thirty; when there were thirty, he dreamed of fifty. Now that there were two thousand to preach to every Sunday, he was dreaming of tens of thousands. He was sure that through a tiny aperture of hope, he was to see new and glorious vistas. According to the image he thought in his head, surely he would become, for God had said it (Prov. 23:7).

Hearts were rehabilitated and homes were put back together. Mental cases came out free from depression and found their place in society.

He chuckled as he walked, recalling the times he had strutted onto the platform practicing to be like the famous American evangelist Billy Graham. He used to memorize the other man's sermons and pray, "Lord, make me like Billy Graham! Make me like Oral Roberts!"

He could almost hear the clear, resounding voice of God: *There is only one Billy Graham. There is only one Oral Roberts. I called you to be Yonggi Cho.*

"But Lord, Yonggi Cho is a nobody."

That's right, son. Not by might, nor by power, but by my spirit, says the Lord.

Spirit. By my spirit says the Lord. That was the mystery and that was the key.

By now Bible school students were making appointments to see the young pastor whose church kept outgrowing the building. "Tell us your secret," they asked.

Answering that the secret was Holy Spirit, he disappointed them every time.

"No, no, not that—we want to know some kind of methods by which you built this," they coaxed.

It was the late sixties. All over the world there was an open restlessness, and student riots and demonstrations from Ohio State to Tokyo. Seoul was no exception. The new morality had set in. Where the rising violence manifested itself in assassinations in one culture, others demanded fingers cut off and sent to official desks. The Bible students wore white shirts and short hair, and aspired to rise higher than either predecessors or peers.

"Well, I have found my ministry," Cho would say. "I'm just a simple vessel of Holy Spirit. At first I didn't accept the position God gave me. I wanted to be a medical doctor. 'I called you to be a pastor,' God said. 'No, make me an evangelist!' I argued.

"So when I finally began to concentrate on pastoring, God gave me the fruit. I have found my ministry. The secret is all in the communion of Holy Spirit. You look at your Bible and see that."

The students turned away as if from a hopeless generation gap. They had not come to hear about Holy Spirit; they had come to hear some practical, sound methodology.

Not unlike the students, Cho had a struggle going on inside him too. He did not have all the answers. While the church was full of common laborers and poor people who had been reborn in the slums and whose lives were revitalized into useful citizens, he felt sure that the city officials, the professionals and the wealthy also suffered the same basic problems as the rest of mankind. Wealthy mothers were as hurt over a child who went astray; fathers of social prestige felt the pressures of society and heavy demands from their positions. He was sure of it. Foreign trade representatives demanded quality; factory foremen, quantity. Stress and strain, worry and fatigue dealt the same essential blows and these were no respecters of persons.

Yet to be heard by the men wealthier than he, to be listened to, Cho was feeling the need for more education. In Korea, two things might be big enough to be heard—age and education. In 1966 he had become general superintendent of the Assemblies of God churches in Seoul and chairman of the board of directors at Full Gospel Bible College. In 1967 he experienced international relationships as he served as a member of the advisory committee of the Pentecostal World Conference. This was the same year that the West Gate church expanded to a five-story front and the *World of Faith (Shinange)* monthly magazine was begun.

In 1968 he graduated from the National College of Korea with a degree in the department of law. That same year he was granted an honorary doctorate, the Doctor of Divinity, from Bethany Bible College in California. He personally preferred using the title "Reverend." Men had called him doctor, but God had called him "pastor."

Cho was careful never to make his appearance on a podium alone. Whether in Germany, France, Scandinavia, America or Australia, he asked Holy Spirit to be his senior partner. In the Bible he had seen that when the early church had a business meeting they wrote into their minutes, "Holy Spirit constrained us . . ." or "Holy Spirit bade us do so-and-so." Hence he felt he was not to put the Holy Spirit in a closet somewhere merely because He was unseen, but to call upon Him, to verbalize His name and lift Him to the position of authority and leadership. Just before a meeting the pastor in his study said, "Okay, Holy Spirit, let's go. I'll work with you and obey your commands, because in this ministry you are my senior partner."

Those commands were not always easy to obey. He felt urged to preach in Japan. "I can't go there. I don't like the Japanese," he reasoned with the Spirit. "I'll go anywhere else, but not Japan." He avoided any flights that would stop in Japan en route. "Anyway, we have a debt of gratitude to repay the West for sending us missionaries; it's our turn now to help them when so much false religion is pouring in from the East." It seemed to be an age of "missions reversed."

In other ways also his Senior Partner was hard to obey. In one meeting in particular a woman sat on the front row in a wheelchair. By the age and wear of her wheelchair, it was obvious she had been a cripple for many years. *Call out to that woman that she is healed, that she can now get up and walk in Jesus' name,* Holy Spirit spoke to Cho's heart. He ignored the impulse. But even as he preached the sermon that evening he was often distracted by visions of various parts of the human body passing before him one by one as if they were on television. He had seen the same type of images before but wondered whether his mind was normal or playing tricks on him.

These things are from Satan, he reasoned. "Why should I see a swollen throat in my imagination at the pulpit? Why should I see twisted ankles and stiff joints? Why even internal organs of the human body as if they are burning up or decaying? Am I going crazy?"

As the meeting was ending and the platform leader directed the congregation in a song, Cho again felt urged to speak to the handicapped woman in the chair. Quietly he walked down the steps and whispered to her, "God wants me to tell you that you can walk. He has touched your body and commands you to stand up and walk."

He hastened away, back to the steps. He had delivered the message. But the crowd started shouting. What was the commotion? Oh, no! The woman was standing up, walking back and forth across the front. The crowd was wild.

Cho was uneasy. Why hadn't he obeyed his Senior Partner in the beginning, if indeed Holy Spirit occupied that position? What right had he to ignore those impulses? He stepped back to the rostrum.

"God loves you and He has performed a miracle. He has also commanded me to speak a word to someone here that you are being healed tonight of a goiter, that you have feared an operation but He is taking away that goiter tonight. You may go back to your doctor tomorrow, and he will tell you that you are well.

"God has also restored someone's deformed legs and when you stand up to walk your twisted ankles will straighten out and be made strong.

"Someone else in this auditorium is suffering from rheumatism and your stiff joints are being made pliable, your pain is being given to Jesus.

"There seems to be a stomach cancer among you, but God has recessed the spread of those decaying cells and His water of life will liquify them again. Jesus has made you whole. Praise God."

One by one, as the various diseases were named, someone would stand up and receive a healing. Kathryn Kuhlman and other healing evangelists had never visited Korea, but these healings were accepted as readily and as naturally as the sicknesses themselves had been accepted.

It was several years later when Cho learned a central truth about the gift of healing from David du Plessis. While some claimed individuals had the gift of healing as described in 1 Corinthians 12, du Plessis suggested that the sick person was given the gift of healing, and the minister was simply like a postman delivering the gift from the Giver. It was a gift for the one who needed it, the ill one who was then made well. In this way no one could glory by serving as postman.

Speak the word, Cho had been urged by the Holy Spirit.

Hadn't the Bible said that whosoever shall speak unto the mountain "Be thou removed, and be cast into the sea," that it should come to pass (Mark 11:23)? Here Jesus had not given instructions to pray, but to speak. There was a time to pray and a time to command.

Being pastor took a heavy toll on his personal life, on his family, and on his draining energy. As the church increased, so did the phone calls in the night. A guilty conscience plagued him whenever he tried to disconnect the phone.

"Pastor, do you know me?" came a man's voice one wintry midnight.

"Yes, I married you and your wife two years ago."

"Our home is no good at all. Tonight we've reached an ultimatum. Tonight we separate! We're already packed up. First thing tomorrow morning I'm filing for divorce. Now, Pastor, since we were married by your blessing, we decided to receive your blessing on our divorce."

"What!"

Finally getting the pastor to agree to come to their apartment, the man hung up and waited.

Pastor Cho likewise sat down in his own living room and waited. For two hours he sat to think without haste. More than the cold outside, another matter delayed his going to the couple's apartment. In his own heart he did not have the faith to assure the couple of any remedy for their problem.

In his mind he was trying to imagine a happy home, trying to create a clear-cut image of them not as the man had described them, but rather as they should be—and with God's help, the man and woman they could actually become. Like an artist sitting before a blank canvas, Pastor Cho smiled and tried to envision the man in a manner opposite from the telephone description a few minutes earlier.

"What are you doing?" the pastor's wife had stolen into the room.

"If that couple has such a terrible problem, how is it that you have such a wonderful smile on your face?" she asked him.

"I'm painting them. Just go back to bed."

From his experience with the bicycle, table and chair during the early days of the tent church, he had tried to be exact when he prayed. He learned from Hee Jae, who could talk now, that a child speaks in plain words when he really wants to ask his father for something in particular, at times pointing so as to be precisely understood. Never did his son utter, "Father, make me happy." Always the child declared in clear-cut words exactly what it would take to make him happy.

In the same way, the pastor began talking to his heavenly Father: "*Abaji* . . ." It was the same word every Korean child used when addressing his own father who could be seen with the eye. "Abaji, in Jesus' name I come to you tonight to ask you to help that couple, Mr. and Mrs.———, living at ————————. You can see them there in their miserable condition. Now I am asking you to make them new. Help me to see the new couple clearly in my mind. . . ."

He prayed and thought, prayed and thought; the difference between this and worrying was that worry centered on the problem, whereas creative praying focused on the solution.

At last when he was inside the couple's apartment, though admittedly uneasy, he walked past the man sitting in the front room, stopped briefly and inquired, "Where is your wife?"

"In there." The man pointed to the bedroom. "Go ahead, you can see her for yourself."

Though the woman stood up to greet him with a sober face, the pastor looked past her face and averted his eyes from the gaping suitcase on the bed. As if to get on with it, he grabbed her hand with one of his and joined the man's hand on his other side as if ready to pronounce a benediction.

"Now, Father, here we are before you—" The couple bowed their heads. In a few minutes Pastor Cho felt a tear fall onto his hand. He opened his eyes. The wife was crying. He looked at the husband's bowed face; the man was fighting back the tears from his eyes too. Taking both their hands from his own, the pastor put the wife's hand into her husband's and shouted in a loud voice that might wake the neighbors: "You spirit of confusion, I command you to leave this place. You depression and bitterness, in Jesus' name I command you to go! Be filled with the love of Jesus Christ, with His peace and beauty now and forevermore. In Jesus' name, be happy! Love each other! Be a successful couple and have a joyful home. Be to yourself and to one another the man and the woman you want to be! In Jesus' name. Amen."

He left.

The following Sunday they both sang in the church choir. "What happened?" the pastor dared to ask the wife after the service.

"We don't know. But when you shouted those commands, we felt something break down in our hearts, like a wall that was shaken, and we needed each other. We spent the rest of that night unpacking our things.

"Now we can't understand why we argued so much, why we were going to separate. It's wonderful. Better than even before!"

Speak the word!
Speak the word!
Speak the word!

That was to become his message for every nation, every pastor, and every believer. *Speak the word!* It was the gospel according to Cho Yonggi. Speak negative faith and reap negative results. Speak sickness, reap sickness. Speak creative words, and reap success. Hadn't God spoken light out of chaos? In the beginning the earth was without form, and darkness was all about. And God said, "Let there be light! And there was light" (Gen. 1:1-3).

And God *said*, and God *said*, and God *said*. It was written all through the Bible. Man was the only part of creation not spoken into being but molded by the hands of God. Man was made in the image of God, the Creator, and because of this, man aches to create. This he must do.

Words energize a man's thoughts. Words are the vehicles of God's plans.

By confession of your mouth, salvation is made unto God (Rom. 10:9-10).

"Speak the word only, and my servant shall be healed" (Matt. 8:8).

"A man hath joy by the answer of his mouth; and a word spoken in due season, how good is it!" (Prov. 15:23).

"The words that I speak unto you, they are spirit, and they are life" (John 6:63).

To activate the promises of God, you must speak the word.

To create the faith for believing it, you must see the goal.

By using his five God-given senses, man could both break the forces that might be against him as well as make the way to successful living.

An athlete first looks directly at the goal, the football player seeing the goal posts clearly before he kicks for the extra point. The basketball player looks at the basket carefully before he shoots, seeing it exactly as it is.

Seeing a clear-cut vision and dream was a principle for success taught in the Bible. God said to Abraham, "For all the land which *thou seest*, to thee will I give it, and to thy seed" (Gen. 13:15). Seeing is the prerequisite for possessing, a formula picked up by advertisers the world over. What the eye sees not, the heart craves not.

Eve *saw* the forbidden fruit and then acted. Lot's wife *looked* back. Seeing can cause trouble as well as blessing; therefore, choosing what to see is definitely a power force for directing one's life or the life of one's children.

When God desired to bless Abraham as the father of the Jewish race, He gave him a visible analogy. "*Look* now toward heaven, and tell the stars, if thou be able to number them: . . . So shall thy seed be" (Gen. 15:5). "And I will make thy seed as the dust of the earth: so that if a man can number the dust of the earth, then shall thy seed also be numbered" (Gen. 13:16).

Moses sent twelve men to *see* the land of Canaan. By their spoken words of fear, ten of them convinced the people to fear and to back away from the original plan of God. Because they said it was difficult, they believed it was difficult. Because the people said they could not conquer the obstacle, then truly they could not. "The men there are so big that we are like grasshoppers next to them," the ten spies said as they painted picturesque words of negative faith (Num. 13:31).

Caleb, on the other hand, gave his report in strong, positive pictures. "It is an exceeding good land. If the Lord delight in us, then he will bring us into this land, and give it us; a land which floweth with milk and honey. Fear not the people of the land; for they are bread for us . . ." (Num. 14:6-9).

From God's instructions and samples given in the Bible, Cho Yonggi was coming to understand the success formula. Think it. See it. Name it. Speak it—in *boldness*. It would work for an athlete, an architect, a housewife, a doctor. The truths about God were not limited to religion; nor should they be limited *by* religion.

It was a formula which he would have the chance to test hundreds of times.

A medical doctor who was a member of Full Gospel Central Church telephoned to say a patient and fellow church member was dying. Though not an old man, the patient was lying unconscious in the hospital; he had been in an unfortunate accident and the doctors had operated and done "all they could do," the phrase which pastors hear universally yet somehow never get used to.

When Pastor Cho walked into the hospital room, a help-lessness came over him as the man lay asleep, unable to respond. "Father, would you please give me five minutes with this man? Can you please wake him up for five minutes so that I can talk to him?"

To his amazement, an eye opened and a weak voice came forth: "Hello, Pastor. My wife—"

"You're going to see her!" he said it like a coach. "Now, close your eyes and paint a picture of yourself. Do you see yourself walking briskly up to your house, with your head up and no pain in your body? You are a fine man, a thoughtful husband and a good father. Your children are jumping on you, and you are very strong. Can you see that man? Can you see him sitting down and eating rice and *kimchi*, and what is that dish over there—some kind of chicken in a sauce? Smells good. Your wife is a tremendous cook, isn't she? Can you see that man?"

By a smile on his face the man in the hospital bed seemed to be responding to the new image being imprinted on his brain. Nurses came and looked, shook their heads and walked away.

The man went back to sleep. Pastor Cho bowed his head and expressed thanks to God before taking his leave.

He could see now why Jesus had put everybody out of the house where Jairus's daughter lay, except a handful of believers. Like the nurses, the people had not understood. Jesus worked side by side with success-minded people (Luke 8:49-56).

The man in the hospital recovered and became a strong pillar not only to his family and the church but to his company and to Seoul. The pastor wondered how much power a family or hospital staff might wield on the extremely ill, even in simple conversations held in the patient's room. It may be erroneous to assume that the sick person cannot hear. Could it be that his will to live might be affected one way or the other by a visitor's remarks?

The power of the spoken word plus the power of a visible goal became a way of life. The church was there not only to meet the needs of the inner man, but to be concerned for body, mind and spirit. To separate these three human parts would be the same as destroying them all.

"Come, follow me and I will make you fishers of men," Jesus had called out to those who would become His disciples. In deep waters, large schools of fish are found, according to Korean fishermen. Hence, Cho's challenge was to launch out into the deep. Life need not be shallow, he thought. Do not separate your Christian life from your secular business, he preached.

Reasoning that God wants people to be prosperous, he described Jesus as a successful businessman. When the disciples had caught nothing after fishing all night, Jesus pointed them to a spot where to cast their nets for one more try. "We've toiled all night and have caught nothing," Simon argued. "Nevertheless, at your word I will let down the net."

When they let down the net as Jesus had directed, they took in so many fish that the net broke, and they had to form a partnership with the men in the other boat (Luke 5:1-11, John 21:3-14). Fishing was not a hobby for them but their line of business.

"I wish above all things that thou mayest prosper and be in health, even as thy soul prospereth," God had said in 3 John 2. Cho used that to encourage his fellow-Koreans to seek the threefold blessing on their finances and their health, as well as their soul. "Seek ye first the kingdom of God and his righteousness, and all these things will be added unto you" (Matt. 6:33).

In trying to fish the people out of the depths of trouble and poverty and provide a new way of thinking and build into them a success-oriented perspective, the church outgrew itself at Sodaemoon.

While praying about how to alleviate the crowded conditions, Cho took on a new idea which he said God told him. He was to relocate and build a church in front of the Congress Hall, to include a seating capacity for 10,000.

"Only government buildings are out there, Lord," he argued. "Anyway, a 10,000-seat building would cost two-and-a-half million dollars!"

In spite of his decade of positive preaching, he was not ready to challenge a two-and-a-half million-dollar debt with only two-and-a-half thousand dollars in the church treasury.

Nevertheless, he called a meeting of the elders. "Pastor, how much money do you propose raising in America?"

"America is not our God, gentlemen. I don't plan to raise any money in America."

"Well, then how much can you borrow from the bank in America?"

"None."

"Pastor, it's a very foolish plan. You're only a preacher, and not a businessman, that's for sure."

With no support from the elders, he called a deacons' meeting. This brought the same results.

"Father," he went to his desk and prayed. "You know we don't have the money to do that."

When did I ask you to build with your money? He felt quickened in his spirit.

"Where is the money, Father?"

I will supply.

"How can I get money from you, God?"

How about your house? If you don't plant something from your hand, how can I multiply it? Where are your five loaves and two fishes?

"My house! I don't have a house. That's my wife's house. I wanted to please her. I could never get permission from her to sell that house."

After a flood in Seoul in 1966, the vice mayor of the city, Il Suk Cha, had been riding in a helicopter to survey the damages and look for ways to help the flood victims and get Seoul back into order. "Wow! Look at that," the words whistled from his lips. "There's a Manhattan down there!"

Having gone through university in New York, Cha suddenly related Manhattan to Yoido, the tiny island off to itself in the flooded Han River, on the outskirts of the city. That helicopter view was the beginning of a city development project which was to change the skyline of Seoul and challenge the world.

Built up from a reclaimed river bed and linked by a bridge to the Seoul metropolis, Yoido became home to Congress Hall, KBS Television, flood control and a sophisticated building code which in turn would lead to more modernization and expansion, bridging the new with the newer, and the present with the future.

It was to Yoido where Pastor Cho's direction was turned. On the nonresidential side of the island, one church would be permitted. Bids poured in from various denominations throughout the nation, all vying for this prestigious location.

Able to get in to see a congressman about it, Cho left the interview feeling relieved that the chances looked impossible. "Assemblies of God?" the congressman had been shaking his head from side to side. "You mean that church where they're loud and where they shout praises to God? That church where they pray for the sick and speak in strange languages?

"You know," he went on, "this church on Yoido is going to be in front of the Congress Hall. Because it will command such a location, it has got to be dignified. And, well, your church is not. We can't accept your application, Dr. Cho."

On his way back to West Gate, Cho figured that that answer would excuse him from launching into the big building program and, no doubt, please the elders and deacons. It would also enable him to avoid an open confrontation with his wife about selling the house.

His fears were not to be averted for long. The next time he sat to pray about it he said with sincerity and confidence, "Lord, you heard that man's answer, didn't you? We're not dignified enough to build out there."

When did I ask you to go and apply for a building permit? the Spirit nudged him.

"Am I not supposed to?"

My child, walk the way of prayer and faith. For we walk

by faith, not by sight (2 Cor. 5:7).

Hanging his head as low as his chin could go, the pastor decided to fast and pray and wait upon his God.

During those days he felt a sure voice inside him, urging him to go and find out who was in charge of the city planning project at Yoido.

After obtaining this information, he further learned the man's mother was a Christian. Like hundreds of other Christians in the city, she regularly worshiped in her church, participating in every way, and then found her way to Full Gospel for an added service in the afternoon.

Encouraged to bring her daughter-in-law, the city official's mother wielded the usual Korean influence of mothers-in-law; and eventually both Cha and his wife made professions of faith and requested baptism.

The next day after he had made his decision for Christ, Il Suk Cha called on Pastor Cho at the church office. "Pastor, I've been thinking. You know, Yoido has sort of become my baby. I'm in charge of the development of the island. We are going to permit one church to come and build there. So I was sort of thinking I wish we could bring this church out there."

Cho wanted to shout! But he played it the Korean way: "No, Vice-Mayor, sir, to bring this church to Yoido would take an enormous amount of money. We would have to buy at least three or four acres of land. Well, that would cost five million dollars, I suppose. Impossible! Anyway, to make matters worse, we are not thought of as a dignified church. We're an undignified Pentecostal church. And so they would not even accept our application."

"I think I have a way," Cha sat on the edge of the chair.

"You pray about it for a week, and then I'll come back; you can give me the answer then.

"Pastor, if you make the decision to move the church there, I'll take care of all the arrangements and handle the paperwork. I'm sure we can fix it up so you could buy the land on credit from the city government."

Cho could not stand it any longer. He just had to shout: "I accept!"

A decision meant more than accepting one thing—it meant cutting away from something else. This decision to move to Yoido was a real plunge, cutting away from having an average-size, comfortable congregation with an average-size, comfortable budget; never would Full Gospel Central Church be average again. Her problems likewise would take on new dimensions. Her image, her needs, her weaknesses and her strengths all would assume new and frightening roles.

The pastor's most frightening job of the moment was to convince his wife that their house was to be given up. "God wants us to plant some seeds," he told her. But even this much he did not say until he had had ample time to compliment her cooking and remind her of how glad he was to have her as his wife.

"What can you plant?"

"House."

Silence.

"What house? This is *my* house. You can't give my house away."

But the die had been cast. Ground-breaking services were held on April 6, 1969, with an 8,000-member nucleus to bear the weight of the future. How true the Korean proverb seemed now: "One generation plants the trees, another gets the shade."

Later Sodaemoon would be given over to Korean Assemblies of God.

"Father, you heard what my wife said about the house," intermittently Cho prayed, still hoping beyond hope that he would somehow be freed from the crazy idea of getting his wife to sell their house for the church. "Father, it's up to you. You are God. You have to do something in her heart. Otherwise, there is no way possible for me to change her mind."

It might have been different had their children been older. Both of them were preschoolers, and boys at that. Samuel was still a baby, able to run around getting into everything. Children needed a place of their own; they needed to feel secure. Sung Hae herself had been from Communist North Korea, uprooted from her home when she was three, following her mother who followed the Navy officer, who followed other women.

She grew restless. At night she began to toss and turn. At meal times she was pensive. Surely she was not pregnant again. Neither Hee Jae nor Samuel had been easy for her to carry.

But this time she was carrying the birth of a building in her thoughts. It was not easy.

One day she quietly put something into her husband's hand, took his other hand in hers for a moment, then folded both his hands around the gift. Papers. Title deed to the house. Her body shook as she cried. Everything they owned was released and given to the God who had given it to them in the first place.

For God had said, "If ye will obey my voice indeed, and keep my covenant, then ye shall be a peculiar treasure unto me above all people: for all the earth is mine" (Exod. 19:5). He had spoken it to His chosen race, the Jews. But the example and the principles, He allowed all nations to enjoy. The fruits of obedience.

The church took five years to build, the Korean nation herself still a developing nation, not yet two decades out of the hovels of war and the aftermath of her separation from the North.

Not only the Han River bridges but the Seoul-Pusan Highway and a network of expressways throughout the nation began to reach out like major arteries in an effort which President Chung Hee Park was to call an all-out national showdown with poverty. There were the "tie wearers" and the "tie haters," and it took one to motivate the other; but most of what went into making modern Korea was not heavy cranes nor electric lifts but the muscles of men, the sinews that held out one stone to another and passed them on, stone upon stone, brick upon brick, shoulder upon shoulder, painful blisters rubbed raw and peeling. A few scabs found their way into the mortar, and a man's sweat-band served as his identity. Rickety wheelbarrows rolled their way through the mud and gravel, hit a snag and overturned and had to be picked up again by the hand that pushed the load.

The church construction, too, hit a snag. The contractor came and broke the contract. He said he had to renegotiate and increase the cost of building the church because of the oil crisis. The banks closed their doors to big loans, and one after another the church members along with others in the city began to lose their jobs. It took the pastor's salary to pay the interest on the previous loans, and the church staff could not be paid.

The construction company proceeded to sue Yonggi Cho for not paying the demands. Notice after notice came in the mail. The church was in arrears with the electric company, the sewage service, the builders. Papers piled up on the pastor's desk. Like Job counting his boils, he could look upon his condition only to add more miseries tomorrow.

Having sold their home and pooled that into the drowning church, they had no place to go. The apartments were not finished but Cho moved his family into a walled-in unit on the seventh floor and called it home. The church had started building a convenient apartment complex next to the gaping hole where the church foundation and basement lay, the iron framework a dinosaur skeleton against the Yoido sky. Sung Hae was pregnant. Frail and weak, she lay upon a mattress to ward off a constant nausea as well as to keep warm in the unheated building. She was not the pioneer woman it would take to haul water up the steps to a seventh-floor flat that had no running water, nor to wag groceries and children up what finally became an open elevator jerkily bumping its way.

The pastor's younger brother had come from Pusan now to attend university, so Yong Chan moved in with his older brother and family.

Cho could see no way to avert failure and utter collapse.

Elders said, "I told you so." Members started dropping out. Rumors went about: "The pastor talks big; he tells us to have faith, but where is his faith now? Let's see him save himself if he can."

He had majored in law but he knew helplessly nothing about lawsuits or banking.

The people seemed somehow to revel in talking about the preacher's troubles. The church members, those who considered them their troubles too, almost enjoyed having miseries. Everyone focused on the ugliness. They forgot to dream. They forgot to rest. Perhaps they had placed their hopes in the man and not in God. That was the most severe of the self-criticisms he could come up with, except that he felt helpless to do anything about it. Like a man overboard, he fought within himself. He fought his children. He fought his wife. Exhausted and tired, he whipped his son Hee Jae until his own hand trembled. He despised his wife; he hated her weaknesses, and cupped his ears when she spoke. At last he hit her. He hit her, and she cried for three days.

At the end of an argument Samuel would walk up and climb silently into his daddy's lap and pat the man's face with his gentle, unwrinkled hand. He never said a word. He did not cry; he did not smile. He patted the man who was his father, and that was all.

Other times Cho Yonggi sat before the window looking out at the barren concrete basement, sometimes the only dry spot on the muddy, rain-drenched lot. A brave few would come to the basement to sing and pray, bringing straw mats to sit on, not unlike the early days at Taejo Dong. But there were no boys out catching frogs "to boil for chicken" any more. When people lived in poverty they did something to satisfy their basic needs, even if it meant catching frogs. But this generation depended on the stores or on the "economy" and in this way they could blame the politicians or someone else for their lot in life.

It was not the first time he had wanted to die. At this moment he could not remember why he had ever wanted to live.

Thud! Dead!

He could hear it in his mind, the sound of his own body hitting the pavement below. Thud! Dead!

He stole away to the fourteenth floor, found a window and crawled to the ledge. It was his only way out.

Not holding on, he prepared to jump.

Suddenly a piece of unfinished work that lay on his desk flashed across his mind and he climbed back into the window and hastened down flight after flight of the unfinished concrete steps, walked straight to his desk and started to work. Like a movie projector running backwards, his mind kept reviewing the incident of his actions moments before. "My big mistake was adding the apartment buildings," he said to himself. His wife had tried to get him not to do it. Holy Spirit had told him to build a church that would seat 10,000; and the pastor had tacked onto it an additional project and called it God's.

"Forgive me, Lord!" he cried out. His wife overheard and knew there was hope.

Why hadn't he jumped? Not a word had been spoken, nor had anyone seen him up there. What was it that had caused his legs to move and carry him back into the window and to the seventh floor? He had not been afraid to die; at that moment it would have been ecstasy. If anything, he was afraid to live.

Elijah, the prophet, had wanted to die, being discouraged

and exhausted, as related in the Old Testament (1 Kings 19:1-8). But an angel had come and touched him and given him food to eat. Cho could not say that he had seen an angel nor heard a sound.

It was not the first time any man had been tempted to jump. Satan had said to Jesus, "Jump!" (Matt. 4:5-6). The same Satan had been saying it to thousands in Asia ever since, especially in Japan where most suicides resulted from jumping off high places; after the war they jumped from cliffs, and today they were jumping from tall buildings or jumping into the path of rushing trains. "Jump!" It was the devil's way. But Jesus had resisted by talking back directly to him, using words that God, the Father, had taught Him.

"Get behind me, Satan!" Cho began speaking aloud as if to a thief who was wielding a weapon. He fought a verbal battle not unlike the one which the youthful David had won over Goliath at the Valley of Elah. The name of Goliath had meant "the exiled one," and like the Hebrews, Koreans believed in the power of names. The Valley of Elah was translated as "strong tree." Throughout Christendom the strongest tree in the world would always be the cross, the point where all men could hang their pasts and stake their futures. "Big debts and lawsuits, you are exiled, you are defeated!" he spoke directly to the problem.

David had said, "I come to thee in the name of the Lord of hosts, the God . . . whom thou hast defied" (1 Sam. 17:45). Yonggi Cho spoke out, "The Lord that delivered me out of the lion's paw of tuberculosis, and out of the bear's paw of influenza, He will deliver me out of the hand of these troubles!" (See 1 Sam. 17:37.)

"Father," he prayed, "I'm sorry for going my own way as if dictating to you what to do. Forgive my stubborn will when it conflicts with your plan. The first thing I want to ask you is to restore my home. . . ." One thought after another swarmed into his mind like bees, and the following Sunday he confessed his obstinacy to the church. A miracle started to happen, the miracle of healing that comes by the release of forgiveness when confessions of faults are made to one another.

The people set out to save their pastor, six hundred to a thousand of them gathering to pray and to offer praise to God in the concrete basement. Each week brought new changes, as an incubative atmosphere was created. The people began to give as much of themselves as they could and in return they themselves somehow had more too. The pastor had no suggestions to make; they did it of their own volition. Women cut their long hair and brought it to the church for making wigs to sell.

From week to week the church offering varied. Counted in with the money donations, there were bus tokens and postage stamps, three or four watches, rings, a banana. It was pieces of themselves that the people gave.

One Sunday a woman in her eighties came making her way steadily to the altar and handed the pastor an old rice bowl, a well-used pair of chopsticks and a spoon. "I want to do something too," she said, "but I have no money except a little pension to keep me going. This is all I have—this old rice bowl, a pair of chopsticks and a spoon. I want to give it all to the Lord's work to help somebody somewhere to know the truth about life. I've decided I can eat out of cardboard and with my fingers."

216

"Oh, Grandmother, I can't accept this from you."
(Grandmother was the customary and polite way of addressing aging women even when they were not related
by family ties.) "It's too much. I know you and I know it's
all you have! You need these things to eat your everyday
meals. In some places people own a Sunday set of dishes
as well as an everyday set, but I know this is your only rice
bowl. I just can't take it."

She began to cry. "You have to take it, Pastor. If Jesus
were here, He would take it. I know it can't help much,
but it's all I have and I want to give something."

Just then a businessman sprang to his feet. "Pastor! I
want to buy those three things!" Tears welled up in his
eyes and his voice broke. He paid almost $30,000 for the
rice bowl, chopsticks and spoon.

It was as if weary travelers upon hot desert sands were
drinking of cool, clear water. Refreshing and life-giving,
the well would never run dry again in the Yoido church.

People began selling their houses and moving into small
apartments. In 1971 the pastor's parents moved from
Pusan to the church apartments at Yoido, along with
over sixty other families in the church. Many young
couples decided to give a year's salary and live by faith.

"Neither was there any among them that lacked: for as
many as were possessors of lands or houses sold them,
and brought the prices of the things that were sold, And
laid them down at the apostles' feet: and distribution was
made unto every man according as he had need" (Acts
4:34-35).

Life savings toward a child's education were brought in
as parents committed the matter to God and taught their

children also to look to God for their futures. Providing educational opportunities for their children was the closest thing to their hearts. Having suffered heavy hardships themselves, parents everywhere determined that their children should have the chance for a good education. For the sake of their children's education, mothers pretended not to want an apple if it meant spending coins which could otherwise be laid aside for a tuition fee or textbooks.

But now children of all ages learned the stark reality of seed planting. This did not involve piling seeds of money up and watching them accumulate in a savings account book, but it involved planting them in the ground for God. Unable to see the seeds at all, they placed their hope in the future and in the plants which would burst forth and yield their seed ten-fold, thirty-fold, a thousand-fold.

Together they were able to pay off the loans and finish building the church and the apartments. The first man who was invited to preach in the new sanctuary was Billy Graham, in 1972. In 1973, the church hosted the Tenth World Pentecostal Conference. Full Gospel Church at Yoido was dedicated on September 24, 1973. Against the rich red and blue decor and enhanced by the spacious blue dome that becomes like a sky of many stars at night, a large blue banner runs all across the front of the auditorium in bold white and gold lettering, in both Korean and English: "IF THOU CANST BELIEVE, ALL THINGS ARE POSSIBLE TO HIM THAT BELIEVETH" (Mark 9:23).

Ten months later associate pastor Jashil Choi founded Prayer Mountain, to which an average of 200,000 from many nations flock annually for prayer and fasting. Some experience fasting for the first time here. On any given day there might be a thousand or more Koreans gathered for prayer on the mountain. When men have a two-week vacation from their company they often take the first week at Prayer Mountain.

In 1974 the church membership reached 23,000; by the close of the decade (1979) it topped 100,000, not including the more than fifty churches that were started in other areas too distant for the people to travel to Yoido.

In 1975 Full Gospel Central Church sent missionaries and established Korean church fellowships in Japan, Europe and the United States and opened a Bible school in Los Angeles especially for those whose English is a second language. In Seoul the church founded a publishing company, separate from the previously started monthly *World of Faith* magazine (*Shinange*).

Dr. Cho was delivering radio broadcasts to reach out with messages of hope and principles of success to all who would dare to seek first the kingdom of God.

In 1977 they dedicated the World Mission Center, ten-story office and dormitory facilities adjacent to the main church building. Church Growth International started conducting a series of international seminars for pastors and church leaders from every continent. By Dr. Cho's invitation, Dr. John Hurston serves as vice-president and dean of Church Growth International.

Holding five worship services every Sunday, Central Church was facing the recurring problem—overcrowded conditions. Certain Christians were requested to alternate their Sundays and stay home at times to allow newer Christians a chance to come inside. With over 7,000 youth packed into one Sunday school department, the department director prayed that the Lord would stop any more from coming; the teachers helped him change his prayer: "Lord, show us how to teach them your ways."

A gymnasium was built, accommodating 2,000 at a time. The people sit on both the seats and the gym floor combined, as the overflow crowd participates in the services via closed-circuit television.

A night school was added, to provide educational opportunities for parents, youth, laborers, or anyone from any strata of society and any age group to continue junior high school or high school training for self-improvement.

A children's magazine is published monthly.

Uniquely Asian, the office of a marriage matchmaker was established in 1978. With so many youth in the church from various backgrounds and social ranks, educational levels and experiences, the services of a go-between would accept applications from both men and women who were seeking a marriage partner; and by their able advice, mature Christians would take the responsibility for this means of improving the nation and society, aiming to establish strong God-centered homes.

A church-education department, newly founded in 1979, became necessary to systematize and develop new materials for Sunday school teaching on all levels.

Keeping abreast of the ever-changing needs of a growing society, the church is adding and shifting like a primary schoolgirl who outgrows her wardrobe for the sophistications of her adolescent years and on toward maturity.

An average of one church member was added every twenty minutes during 1978.[23]

The next main auditorium would double the former

seating capacity of 10,000.

By now the Lord's Supper, commemorated once every month, required truckloads of grapes for making the wine, and vats of pounded rice for making the "bread" which looked perhaps like the white manna of Moses' day. Women of the church once a year washed and selected the firm round grapes and prepared them for their patient two-year fermentation in twelve clay vessels, tall and heavy, buried in the ground in the cellar beneath the church. One of the twenty-four jars was brought out each month, diluted with water and served in the thousands of tiny individual cups, reverently reminding the individual believers in each service of the life of Christ. "This cup is the new testament in my blood, which is shed for you," Jesus had said (Luke 22:20). Likewise the bread was a symbol: "This is my body which is given for you: this do in remembrance of me" (Luke 22:19). While some churches use juice in the sacrament, Pastor Cho preferred to avoid the chemical preservatives in modern canned juice and allow the wine, weak though it was, to seal the remembrance and celebration of this blood covenant between man and God, and to demonstrate the brotherhood of men.

The 100-voice choirs and the orchestra combine with trumpets and the many thousands of worshipers lift praises to God, and the joyful praise resounds all over that part of Yoido. Some of the best musicians and orchestra directors of Korea participate in the music, mixing catchy Scripture choruses with high cantatas. In keeping with Korean taste for hymns and high-church style, the overflowing congregation closes each service by singing

"The Lord's Prayer" in Korean, accompanied by rolling timpani, enriched by the many strings of violins and cellos, and carried higher by cornets ringing out together: "Our Father which art in heaven, Hallowed be thy name. Thy kingdom come. Thy will be done in earth, as it is in heaven. Give us this day our daily bread. And forgive us our debts, as we forgive our debtors. And lead us not into temptation, but deliver us from evil: For thine is the kingdom, and the power, and the glory, forever. Amen."

9

Come Home, Your Son Is Dying!

(1978-1980)

The woman was thin and emaciated. Her cheeks were sallow, her eyes looked downward and her expression was empty. Her husband had brought her to the church office.

Every case was different. How to deal with each one in their differences, how to see each individual as a unique creation of God and not necessarily like the other thousands in the church—this was a constant challenge to the pastor. He must have discernment, the discernment that could come only from a close relationship with the God who knew them—the God who knew every one by name.

The church staff developed a system whereby every church member was catalogued and cross-referenced. On a moment's notice it was possible for the pastor to be handed a photo and description of any individual and that person's family. Not unlike a doctor briefing himself on a patient's medical history, the pastor could quickly be prepared to counsel anyone who came to him. It was important to be able to ask about one's children by name, to congratulate one on a recent achievement on the job or in the community. It was important that the shepherd know the name of every sheep.

Even so, discernment was the key. "To separate apart" like panning for gold, it was necessary to discern the good in a person which could be refined and lifted above whatever filth should be left behind.

"Tell me your past," he said to the woman after excusing her husband to wait in another room.

"What is this—the police station?" she retorted.

But soon she spilled the whole story. She had had an affair with her brother-in-law when her sister went to the hospital to have a baby. Now she felt guilty whenever she lay in bed with her own husband. She had had abortions, and she felt guilty that her three children loved her.

"I can never be forgiven!" she said with her eyes and mouth set.

"What now, Lord?" Cho prayed out loud for an idea. "Close your eyes," he instructed. "Let's go to a quiet and beautiful lake. You and I are sitting beside the lake, the water blue and still. Now, in my hand I hold a small pebble. There are a lot of pebbles all around. You pick up one too—you pick up a big rock, if you will. Got it?

"Now let's throw this pebble and this rock into the lake. Ready?

"First, it's my turn. I have the pebble in my hand and now I throw it in. Did you hear the sound it made? Did you see the ripples in the lake? Where is my pebble now?"

The lady responded, "Well, it went down to the bottom

of the lake."

"Right. Now it's your turn. Cast your rock in. There it goes. Did it make a noise like the pebble?"

"No, it made a big splash! And wide ripples," she answered.

"But where is your rock now?" Cho asked.

"Down at the bottom."

"Well, it seems that my small pebble and your big rock both went to the bottom of the lake when they were tossed. The only difference was the sound and the ripples. Mine made a plop and yours made a boom. People go to hell with small sins just as well as large sins, because they don't cast their sins away on Jesus Christ, the water of life. And what is the difference? Only their sound and their influence on society.

"The Bible says, 'If we confess our sins, he is faithful and just to forgive us our sins, and to cleanse us from all unrighteousness' (1 John 1:9).

"In the same way that you cannot see that stone any more, you can be free from this awful guilt by simply asking Jesus to forgive you, then you can just go on and live your life and hold your head up, sing songs to God, and enjoy your husband and children. That's why Jesus had to die, to set *us* free—free from the messes we get ourselves into. It is the world that says, 'You made your bed, now lie in it.' That's where Jesus' way is different."

She prayed with her own words a simple list of the things she had felt guilty for and called on the name of Jesus to help her. Then they started to sing a song on the goodness of God, and a glimmer of light came into the woman's eyes. Her husband was amazed when he came back into the room and his wife looked up at him smiling. Her eyes had not met his in a long time.

Central Church had started out with two members, then five. Now that it was on its way to a hundred thousand, one thing would always remain the same—the basic human needs of every individual—the need for love, for security, for creative expression, for recognition, for new experiences, and for self-esteem.

When the church had grown at Sodaemoon, assistant pastor, Jashil Choi, began to section off the city as a means of reaching out to every district in Seoul. "The life . . . is in the blood," it was written in Leviticus 17:11. Hence, the lifeblood of the church body representing the atonement of Christ must be pumped through every artery into every vein and to the tiniest capillary throughout the city. Human needs had to be met in the neighborhood, and at home, where the people lived and functioned. It would be crazy to think of a liver having to come up to the heart to receive its supply of blood that gave it life; the toe, the ear, the stomach, all the body parts functioned where they were and did not suffer lack of the same life-giving blood. Like the blood that circulated throughout every fiber of the human body every twenty-three seconds, there must be constant renewal and regular contact flowing through the wealthy who lived in high-rise brick houses as well as through the simplest people who lived in a tiny room somewhere.

By trial and error, and by the readiness to change a method if it needed changing, a network of city-wide service was begun which activated over 7,000 small groups by 1979, each with trained but unpaid leaders who could be called on at any time. Over a cup of tea, women shared their problems and prayed regularly for their children and their husbands; men became more successful in their business and youth found their nooks in society; school examination scores improved; and sicknesses decreased.

All growing matter had life, and all living matter had growth. On the back side of every leaf there could be observed the same pattern, for the life is in the blood. The life-giving sap was flowing through arteries, veins, capillaries, branching off and winding to the very tips and outer edges of every leaf to give it green. If all was well at the grass roots, there was no need to worry about the color of the meadow.

As a biological cell tissue grows by splitting in two, it was necessary to split the neighborhood cell groups from time to time. Five to ten homes held a week-night time of praise and prayer as well as Bible study at a time and house convenient to those neighbors involved. When the group expanded to fifteen households, a district overseer recommended that two cells be formed, because in the small groups each person could participate and come into spiritual health and maturity.

"And they, continuing daily with one accord in the temple, and breaking bread *from house to house*, did eat their meat with gladness and singleness of heart, Praising God, and having favor with all the people. And the Lord added to the church daily such as should be saved" (Acts 2:46-47).

The church staff involved one hundred twenty associate pastors and almost 5,000 deacons and deaconesses, not to mention the lay leadership and heads of various departments. (For details on the church organizational structure, the cell system, leadership training seminars, and publications available in English, write to Dr. John Hurston or Karen Hurston, c/o Church Growth International, Full Gospel Central Church, Yoido P.O. Box 7, Seoul, Korea.)

The associate pastors all met together with the pastor every morning before dispersing throughout the city or the church offices to carry out their work for the day. The meeting was not a planning session but a devotional time.

The Central Church functioned primarily as a training center, especially training the laity. Video TV was put to use as in their spare time the Bible women as well as the other home cell leaders were trained each week. Eventually a personalized teaching corps was built up, so that the church was alive with constant teaching and learning and learners became teachers.

Within the church family there were some who preferred close-family weddings or small-village funerals, while others requested large public occasions. For a church that buried 150 members a year, this function also must be as personalized as possible. The whole church body served and circulated, ever mindful of the joys and the sorrows of one another as well as those of the non-members who were part of their own neighborhoods, quietly sharing with each other, be it in a financial pinch or some other personal and natural ways of life. "I need a little help on my son's tuition" plus "you need help putting in the zipper in your daughter's dress" meant that two could become one; and this multiplied by 100,000 drew them together toward the One who was their center, that is Christ, their example and their energy, their motivation and their goal. Koreans had grown up bearing brothers on their backs.

Men who opened a shop for themselves, men from the large company, the factory, the pastry shop or the smallest stationery store—all held an opening prayer meeting, inviting the pastor or an associate pastor to speak and to pray for God's blessings on the business. Weekly prayer and Bible times are common to hotel personnel who are Christians; such times are common at train stations during lunch breaks, and school campuses before classes begin.

Among South Korea's population of 36,628,485 (as of October 1, 1978) there was a Christian population of 7,115,000, dispersed among 19,236 churches. (As the born-again rate is four times the population birth rate in Korea, these figures are subject to rapid change.) The Koreans who have seen the destruction of accumulated material goods and life savings have transferred their emphasis to the spiritual and to the hope of eternal life: "Lay not up for yourselves treasures upon earth, where moth and rust doth corrupt, and where thieves break through and steal: But lay up for yourselves treasures in heaven, where neither moth nor rust doth corrupt, and where thieves do not break through nor steal: For where your treasure is, there will your heart be also" (Matt. 6:19-21).

In international leadership conferences, Dr. Cho has been asked time and time again the secret of the large church phenomenon. "Well, who can say?" he confessed before a TV audience one day. "It is only the moving of God in His mercy—God's timing for Korea."

He specifies all or part of the following ten categories as factors which gave birth to the church and keep it healthy. These are seen as keys to successful life: (1) Holy Spirit; (2) Prayer, including frequent all-night prayer and regular early morning prayer; (3) Fasting; (4) Organization, delegating leadership of lay people, especially mobilizing women; (5) Dare to dream a clear-cut goal and vision in order to create the desired image; (6) Speak the word in boldness, bringing the dream into existence by the power of the spoken word; (7) Obedience to the Lord; (8) Clear confession of faults before God, the acceptance of His forgiveness and in turn personal forgiveness of self and others; (9) Success-mindedness, success-oriented friends; and (10) Receptivity.

As part of his success formula, he has often been quoted on the following points:

The world is sick and tired of hearing about Jesus Christ—now they want to experience Him.

God wants us to be prosperous and successful.

Love is the ultimate answer.

Hatred, fear, inferiority complex, and guilt—these four are at the heart of broken lives and homes, and the root of a man's failures.

Man should not waste anything. After Jesus fed the crowd, the twelve disciples went around and gathered up the leftovers.

Start small, then grow big.

If God gives a man a healing ministry, one must never charge money for those services nor use it to seek private gain.

Be generous. Give to others. Bless others.

Women make effective teachers and are diligent and faithful. When Christ was crucified, all the men left, but the women remained until the last moment.

Seventy percent of those going to hospitals today could be cured if the churches would do their job.

If a person receives Christ and His love, that person can become a more creative, positive, productive, progressive and happy person.

To one who has much, much will be required.

Be still, and know that God is God.

The West was said to be "male" in its thinking—practical, logical and progressive. Eastern thought was "female," or emotional, intuitive and passive. Cho thought that somewhere the two must mix, for the perpetuation of the church in this day when travel and trade have helped to bring the world together as one household.

His mother-in-law had been after him for years to go and preach in Japan and to pray for the Japanese. Still harboring hatred and bitter childhood memories, he avoided the subject. Many years earlier he had felt Holy Spirit calling him to Japan to share the ideas on successful living as taught in the Bible. By all outward appearances the Japanese were successful, yet he had heard of the great inner struggles in the heart of students, and even in the homes.

Seeing his mother-in-law weep as she prayed for "the wonderful Japanese" who had not seen the light of Jesus' love, and the frustrating social demands on the "lovely" Japanese, he tried to mumble off a prayer in their behalf but he just didn't have it in him. He knew he *should* love his neighbors, but he could not muster up love for them from any direction he turned. He read again the world's most famous words about love:

If I speak with the tongues of men and of angels, but do not have love, I have become a noisy gong or a clanging cymbal.

And if I have the gift of prophecy, and know all mysteries and all knowledge; and if I have all faith, so as to remove mountains, but do not have love, I am nothing.

And if I give all my possessions to feed the poor, and if I deliver my body to be burned, but do not have love, it profits me nothing.

Love is patient, love is kind, and is not jealous; love does not brag and is not arrogant,

does not act unbecomingly; it does not seek its own, is not provoked, does not take into account a wrong suffered,

does not rejoice in unrighteousness, but rejoices with the truth;

bears all things, believes all things, hopes all things, endures all things.

Love never fails; but if there are gifts of prophecy, they will be done away; if there are tongues, they will cease; if there is knowledge, it will be done away.

For we know in part, and we prophesy in part; but when the perfect comes, the partial will be done away.

When I was a child, I used to speak as a child, think as a child, reason as a child; when I became a man, I did away with childish things.

For now we see in a mirror dimly, but then face to face; now I know in part, but then I shall know fully just as I also have been fully known.

But now abide faith, hope, love, these three; but the greatest of these is love. (1 Cor. 13:1-13 NAS)

His mother-in-law prayed for him, specifically that he would come to love the Japanese, that he would release them by forgiving Japan, and that war memories would be healed by the soothing oil of Holy Spirit throughout Asia. By unforgiveness Korea had the power to bind Japan from spiritual blessings and true happiness in life. Jashil Choi fasted and prayed for the Japanese and for her son-in-law.

In 1973 when the All-Japan Pentecostal Conference invited him as their speaker, he could hardly refuse. The meetings went on with no particular crisis and no particular merit, several hundred pastors and church leaders gleaning fresh ideas from a fellow Asian.

In the final session with no plan of doing so, Yonggi Cho stood before them and opened his heart. "I have an apology to make," his voice spoke softly. "All this week I have preached to you but I hated you. I did not wish to ever set foot on Japanese soil because of the terrible memories I hold in my heart, and the rape of my country.

When God first spoke to me about coming to minister in Japan, I refused. I am not proud of my sin of disobedience nor my sin of hatred. And so I ask your forgiveness for my hypocritical attitude before you these few days. I used to reason that the Japanese deserved hell. But the mercy of God makes us equal."

Grown men wept.

But most of the preachers had not gone to war; most of them had been boys, some of them in the last junior high class of fourteen-year-olds whose turn was next to be inducted but whose turn never came because the war ended. Many of the Japanese in the audience that day had only vague ideas of the life in Japan-occupied territory throughout Asia, as the history books had powdered-over the scar. They had not really known the bleeding truth nor the ugly scabs. It was not Cho's purpose to tell them. He told them only about the church that he had seen the soldiers burn down full of people, poking the baby back into the flaming building. It was an impression which he was never quite able to erase.

The Japanese began to love the Korean man that day, and a strange thing happened as he made his way out of the meeting place and back to the city. He longed to know them better. He longed to laugh with them and to eat Japanese food with them. He longed to refresh his Japanese and be able to communicate man-to-man without the need for an interpreter. His mother-in-law had been praying for that too.

Every year he has been invited back to either teach in leadership conferences or conduct crusades. He got a Japanese Bible in order to study the language again. And a

234

large map of Japan adorns his desk under a glass top, serving as his visual aid to a clear-cut vision and dream, aiding him to pray more specifically for Japan.

"You are the leaders of Asia," he told them. "You are exporting calculators, tape recorders, cars and cigarettes all over the world. You should be exporting the message of Jesus Christ, the Truth about life. You have the television know-how for doing this, you have all the latest equipment, technology and resources—the gospel in Asia depends on you Japanese!" he challenged. "You have the finances, the freedom, and the responsibility.

"For the cause of the Empire your slogan used to be 'The World One Household.' For the cause of the peace and love of Jesus Christ, it is in your hands—The World One Household!"

The threat of Communist aggression and guerrilla warfare is constant in South Korea, as the South Koreans experience infiltrations and raids from time to time from the North. Hence, the people pray for Japan and surrounding nations to remain healthy and free from the cancer of Communist control.

Every Saturday afternoon, when he is at home, Cho goes to his private grotto at Prayer Mountain, spending hours in solitude and quiet, waiting on the Lord. Sunday preaching is never mere routine for him but this is the most serious of all his work. More important than making a good speech is touching the people directly where they are in their thought life and in their everyday world. There are times when Koreans need encouragement and need to be built up, to be lifted into believing in themselves and to be shown personal worth.

He had read sermons from the West, where it seemed the emphasis was on how lowly man is, how sinful and unworthy, and he had heard the song go on about "what a worm am I." On the other hand, Cho felt that the Koreans naturally condemned themselves, wore self-pity and an inferiority complex. They needed to see themselves as creative beings in the likeness of a creative Father. He thought there must be a fine line between being humble and being self-degrading and damaging.

There was no better place to prepare for the next day's sermons than on his knees at Prayer Mountain. Over 200 one-mat caves had been dug into the mountain like catacombs, each equipped with a door and ventilation, and large enough for one to stand up or lie down. In cold weather the people brought blankets and stayed for several days fasting and praying. When the grottoes were all being used, 800 to 1,000 could sit on the chapel floor of the main building on the mountain. Dormitory facilities were also available, along with a dining area for anyone in a partial fast or for someone new at fasting who went into it gradually and came out of it on a liquid diet. (For Jashil Choi's teachings on fasting and prayer, write for her book, *Korean Miracles*, c/o Young San Publishers, Full Gospel Central Church, Yoido P.O. Box 7, Seoul, Korea.)

When his mother-in-law first started Prayer Mountain, she had two reasons for seriously involving Christians everywhere in fasting prayer: (1) sickness and (2) materialism. "While medicine was developed to be our servant," she said, "we have become its slaves."[24]

She further believed that, like herself at one time in her life, people were too involved with material gain and that their lives, as a result, became devoid of meaning and purpose.

Her husband had come back to her feeling the same way. After ten years of separation, they put their home back together and his life took an about-face. Baptized John Kim, he went to Bible school and became his son-in-law's assistant for several years until his death.

In some years when the pastor traveled an equivalent of half a year, his growing concern was what man the Lord would call to the pulpit in his absence. The preacher turned out to be Yong Mok Cho, his own brother eight years younger than he. Yong Mok was the baby brother who could hardly get his breath during a siege of the whooping cough, causing Yonggi to run into his room to pray, "God above all the gods, will you please make my brother live!" (Refer to page 51.)

Another concern was his own given name. His name continued to be a problem when he traveled to Europe or America. After some experimenting, he finally took the name "Paul" for foreign use, although in Korea a man was recognized for his role or occupation rather than his individuality. In the East a person was not known by his own name but as "so-and-so's father," "Mr. Section Chief," "Teacher," "Pastor," "Pastor's Wife," etc. It added to one's sense of direction and single-mindedness.

Paul of the New Testament was a tent maker, so it seemed that a Korean church builder might have a definite kinship with him. He could clearly remember when God had spoken to him through Isaiah the prophet: "Enlarge the place of thy tent, and let them stretch forth the curtains of thine habitations: spare not, lengthen your cords, and strengthen thy stakes; for thou shalt break forth on the right hand and on the left" (Isa. 54:2-3).

Paul also had a certain amount of boldness about him; and Cho often said if he himself had any gift from the Lord, it was boldness and nothing more.

The double g-sound in the middle of "Yonggi" seemed strange for Westerners to say; but a softer pronunciation of "Yongi" would render the meaning "dragon" instead of "boldness or courage." Anyway, it would simply be too strange for him to be addressed by his own name. Surely if a foreign visitor to Korea should ever address him with "Yonggi," fellow-Koreans would misunderstand and think the guest uncivilized or crude. No, it would be better to be Paul.

He wished he could speak better English, and there were often things he wished afterwards he had not said or that he had not done. It seemed that when he would overcome in one area he would fall down in another. But he had to take God at His Word and move on. It never ceased being a mystery to him how the God of all creation would use the weak things to confound the strong. And he was eternally grateful for this. Riding in the car en route to other cities or to other points within Seoul, he often communicated quietly with God. "Father, Father!"

"Thank you, Jesus."

"Wonderful Jesus!"

It was a sort of relaxant. These and "Father, Father" slipped most frequently from his lips. When tired or when fully rested and feeling his best, it didn't matter—one of those three phrases would slip from his lips.

He loved to ride in the car, the driver being either quiet

or jovial, whichever mood the pastor seemed to need. It was a time to think. In the doing of anything big, it was an absolute must to take time for thinking, time for dreaming. "Rise above your busy schedules," he said to men everywhere. "Dare to dream."

He said it because he believed it; he believed it because it worked. It could lift a nation from the depths of despair, and it could lift men or women to the victorious living which he believed the Bible was guiding them to enjoy.

The Bible had preserved the Korean *Hangul* writing system at a time in Korean history when the language was about to be rejected for its simplicity. In a day when learned men wanted to keep the commoners illiterate, the complicated Chinese writing system was preferred with its thousands of characters and many strokes. Ironically some Christians in China printed Bible portions in *Hangul*, which any and every Korean could read, and brought the books across the borders into the then-closed hermit nation. It was a message of Jesus, a message of man's victory over himself, a message for every person.

"Come home immediately. Our son is dying!"

His wife's emergency telephone call had come to a men's meeting downtown where he is was speaking. It was the end of 1978. Dying? Which boy could it be? Hee Jae was in junior high school, Samuel and Sung Jae were in primary school. There must be some mistake; that morning they had all three been fine.

After weaving and inching its way through the Seoul traffic, the black sedan finally arrived at their apartment.

Cho found his wife frantic and helpless. Samuel was lying asleep on his father's bed, and by now he could not be awakened. Before dropping into such a deep sleep he had said to his mother, "Tell Daddy to pray for me." Then rolling his head on his pillow he added, "But I'm pretty sure I'm going to heaven tonight."

Doctors were working late all over the city, it seemed. Cho, taking off his tie and shoes, cried out, "Father, Father," as he dialed another doctor. "Well, it's no use, Pastor. Eight boys have died tonight already. There is really not anything any of the doctors can do for Samuel now. It's too late. If he is in that sleep like you say, then it won't be long now; he won't suffer any more; he will go in peace. Pastor. Pastor."

Go in peace? Samuel was his son who had loved him and patted him with his gentle baby hands. "No, Lord, not Samuel! Not yet!"

Something the boys had eaten on their way home from school had been dipped in poison and they ate it unaware.

Cho and his wife had dared to name their second son Samuel because of a dream which revealed to Sung Hae that she was pregnant and carrying a son. She had been sick day after day, never suspecting another pregnancy yet, not after the first one had been so difficult. Even the doctors had not diagnosed her trouble. But one night she dreamed about an Old Testament woman named Hannah, and then she herself appeared in the dream with Hannah, and she heard a voice speak to her: "In your belly there is a boy, and his name is Samuel." At breakfast she and her husband had laughed over it, but Sung Hae often dreamed complete songs in her sleep and she could write them down and set them to music the next day.

After this dream she had gone back to the doctor, who confirmed she was indeed expecting another baby. Breaking all Korean tradition, they named him Samuel, a name which he had faced for its strange differences at school. Just as a boy does not really want his father to be different from other boys' fathers, neither does he himself want to be too different. But Samuel had managed. And he had a lot of friends.

In true Korean style it was customary to give every son a special generation name. Hence, all of Cho's brothers had been named Yong something: Yong Gi, Yong Ou, Yong Mok, Yong Chan, and Yong Bae. It was expected that Yonggi's sons must all bear *Jae* as the second part of their given name; therefore Hee *Jae* and Sung *Jae*. In turn, the sons of these sons are to inherit *Rae* as the second part of their name, followed the next generation by *Hyun* as the first sound in the name. A girl might rarely be honored with a brother's generation name.

Samuel alone had no generation name to bestow on a future offspring. But why should he not be allowed to inherit the future? "No, Samuel! You cannot go away yet!" his father cried out beside the bed.

Then crawling to the middle of the bed, sitting in stockinged feet beside the lifeless body, Cho began to pray. "Father, I will not let my boy go!"

It was hard to pray. Words sounded hollow and useless. If he had not seen Samuel stretched out upon the bed, he thought he could come nearer praying. It was too big a contrast to see the stark reality of the condition before him, yet try to muster up contrary words of hope. The boy's mother had been praying all evening constantly beside him.

The man beside his boy had only one choice, to close his eyes and try to focus on the healthy, robust image he remembered Samuel to be. "Father, Father!" Still he couldn't pray. Samuel was a sportsman in Tae Kwondo (a Korean art of self-defense), and a well-rounded boy; the leader of the pack, he had eaten more of the deep-fried silkworms than any of the other boys. In Korea at a certain cocoon or eggshell stage the silkworm was a fine and delicious treat; fathers often stopped by a fry-vendor's place to take a bag home for their children to enjoy eating. But this afternoon, the farmer who had brought the catch into town had put them into an empty bag for carrying them and the bag had contained a strong insecticide used on the farm crops. According to the doctors, it seemed that everyone who ate at that certain vendor's today had died in the night.

"Father, forgive me, the father of this boy. Forgive me for. . . ." And he went on praying, naming one wrong after another that he had done or thought. For an hour, for two hours, he prayed, not in generalities but for exact sins of his own which he recalled, for times he had wronged his wife in word or deed, his ingratitude for his children, etc. "Create in me a clean heart, O God; and renew a right spirit within me" (Ps. 51:10).

When the man opened his eyes again, Samuel appeared to have no life left in him. No one could rouse him or communicate with him in any way.

"Father, I call upon your grace and mercy to please,

please let Samuel stay here with us. We are not worthy that such a favor should be granted to us, but we beg you, out of your kindness and love, to restore Samuel to the vigorous and healthy boy you made him to be."

He went on praising God past midnight, still sitting cross-legged on the bed. But he could not look at the body beside him, too silent and too still. To look upon it took away all his incentive to pray.

"Father, I see him now tall and strong, jovial, running up the steps at church two at a time; now he's trying three at a time; he jumps into the air twisting his body like a graceful athlete to shoot a field goal. . . ."

After a while he got off the bed, stood facing the boy and in a thundering voice commanded, "Samuel!"

He clapped his hands together in a loud, jolting manner. "Samuel! In the name of Jesus Christ of Nazareth, rise up and walk!"

The boy sprang to his feet!

Cho bolted backwards in fear.

Samuel crumpled and fell halfway across the bed, vomiting upon the sheets.

His mother bent to bathe his face, but she was almost afraid to touch him too soon. Samuel spoke and gestured with his hand. "Say hello to Jesus, Papa."

He said it again. "Say hello to Jesus. He's right there." The boy pointed.

Going along with his son's strange talking, Cho bowed politely toward the space where the boy had indicated and said softly, "Hello, Jesus."

"Didn't you see us coming down the hallway? Didn't you see us, Papa? Jesus carried me in His arms like this."

Both voice and gestures were weak but the parents could make out his words perfectly.

"Jesus was carrying me next to His chest to a *beautiful* place." He stretched out the word along with his hand.

"It was bright, brighter than anything I've ever seen. All the colors of the world are dull next to those colors He showed me.

"And music! Mama, you'd love it too. It was the most beautiful music my ears have ever heard. I couldn't recognize the tune, but we kept getting closer and closer to it.

"Then Jesus said to me, 'We have to go back.'"

"'No,' I said. 'Yes, we have to go back. Your father won't let you go.'

"And He was bringing me in here to the bedroom. Didn't you see us coming down the hall?

"You were calling me, and you commanded me to get up. That's when Jesus let go of me. There He is—oh, He's not there. He must have gone back, I guess."

I go to prepare a place for you.
And if I go and prepare a place for you,
I will come again,
and receive you unto myself;
that where I am, there ye may be also.
And whither I go ye know,
and the way ye know.
I am the way, the truth, and the life:
no man cometh unto the Father, but by me.
Because I live, ye shall live also.
The Comforter, which is the Holy Ghost,
whom the Father will send in my name,
he shall teach you all things,
and bring all things to your remembrance,
whatsoever I have said unto you.
Peace I leave with you, my peace I give unto you:
not as the world giveth, give I unto you.
Let not your heart be troubled: neither let it be afraid.
I go unto the Father: for my Father is greater than I.
And now I have told you,
that ye might believe.

Jesus

Notes

[1]Post Wheeler, *Dragon in the Dust.* The Marcel Rodd Company: Hollywood, 1946, p. 95.

[2]Unofficial, general wording based on reports from several Korean men as they remember it.

[3]In the United States, President Harry S. Truman announced at 7:00 P.M. Eastern Standard Time, Tuesday, August 14, 1945, that Japan had accepted the terms to end the war. Japan being further east and therefore a day ahead of the U.S. time zones, the Emperor's pre-recorded announcement came at noon on August 15, Japan Standard Time. This is how Koreans and Japanese remember it as well as how it is recorded in the newspaper files there. Thus August 15 became the Korean national holiday, Liberation Day.

[4]Leonard Mosley, *Hirohito: Emperor of Japan.* Englewood Cliffs: Prentice-Hall, Inc., 1966, p. 355.

[5]*Ibid.,* p. 347.

[6]The Chinese "Yin-Yang" theory, known in Korea as "Um-Yang."

[7]*Korea, Its Land, People and Culture of All Ages.* Hakwon-sa, Ltd., Seoul: 1960.

[8]Rutherford M. Poats, *Decision in Korea.* The McBride Company: New York, 1954, p. 337.

[9]Lao Tzu, *Tao Te Ching* (Translated by D.C. Lau), Penguin Books Ltd., Baltimore: 1963, p. 140.

[10]*Ibid.,* p. 125 .

[11]*Ibid.,* p. 110.

[12]Hugh MacMahon, *The Scrutable Oriental.* Sejong Corporation Publishers, Seoul: 1975, p. 25.

[13]William Shakespeare, *The Tragedy of Hamlet, Prince of Denmark.* Act II, Scene 2, line 316.

[14]John Donne, "The Tolling Bell—A Devotion."

[15]Hermann Hesse, *The Glass Bead Game.* (Translated from German to English by Richard and Clara Winston.) Holt, Rinehart and Winston, New York: 1969, pp. 58-59.

[16]Hermann Hesse, *Beneath the Wheel.* Translated by Michael Roloff. Bantam Books, Inc., New York: 1968, p. 162.

[17]Hermann Hesse, *Demian.* Translated from German to English by Michael Roloff and Michael Lebeck. Harper & Row, Publishers: New York, 1965, p. 94.

[18]S.I. McMillen, M.D., *None of These Diseases.* Fleming H. Revell Company, Old Tappan, New Jersey: 1977, pp. 64-65.

[19]F.A. McKenzie, *Korea's Fight for Freedom.* Yonsei University Press: Seoul, 1969, p. 199.

[20]*Ibid.*, p. 247-249.

[21]Cornelius Osgood, *The Koreans and Their Culture.* The Ronald Press Company: New York, 1951, p. 287.

[22]Hermann Hesse, *Beneath the Wheel.* (Translated from German to English by Michael Roloff.) Bantam Books, Inc., New York: 1953, p. 58.

[23]Karen Hurston, Editor, *World of Faith* English Edition. Full Gospel Central Church, Seoul: Spring, 1979, Vol. 1, No. 1. Page 14.

[24]Jashil Choi, *Korean Miracles.* Mountain Press: La Canada, California, 1978, p. viii.

DREAM YOUR WAY TO SUCCESS

Suggested Reading
Other Church Growth Titles from Logos

Fourth Dimension by Dr. Paul Yonggi Cho. (P380-6) Dr. Cho shares the principles of faith which God has helped him to understand. "Put your faith in Jesus Christ and expect a miracle today," Dr. Cho tells us.

Cells for Life by Ron Trudinger. (P416-8) A positive solution and recommendation for churches desiring to grow. A "how-to" book for home fellowships, cell groups and churches interested in "share and care" in homes.

The Exploding Church by Tommy Reid with Doug Brendel. (P299-8) Tommy Reid tells how his ministry intensified when he followed his vision from the Lord. His testimony is a challenge to all church members.

Miracle in Darien by Bob Slosser. (P427-5) With the careful eye of a journalist, Bob Slosser gives us the story of a remarkable experiment in faith—how the rector and his people decided to let Christ be the true head of their church. The results were miraculous.